ISBN 978-0-484-39783-4
PIBN 10115758

THE SEVENTH YEARBOOK

OF THE

NATIONAL SOCIETY FOR THE SCIENTIFIC STUDY OF EDUCATION

PART I

THE RELATION OF SUPERINTENDENTS AND PRINCIPALS TO THE TRAINING AND PROFESSIONAL IMPROVEMENT OF THEIR TEACHERS

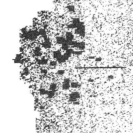

THIS YEARBOOK WILL SERVE AS THE BASIS OF DISCUSSION AT THE WASHINGTON MEETINGS OF THE NATIONAL SOCIETY, ON MONDAY, FEBRUARY 24, AT 7:45 P. M., AND WEDNESDAY, FEBRUARY 26, AT 4:30 P. M.

CHICAGO
THE UNIVERSITY OF CHICAGO PRESS
1908

The Seventh Yearbook

OF THE

NATIONAL SOCIETY FOR THE SCIEN-TIFIC STUDY OF EDUCATION

PART I
THE RELATION OF SUPERINTENDENTS AND PRINCIPALS TO THE TRAINING AND PROFESSIONAL IMPROVE-MENT OF THEIR TEACHERS

BY
CHARLES D. LOWRY
District Superintendent of Schools, Chicago, Illinois

EDITED BY
MANFRED J. HOLMES
Illinois State Normal University, Normal, Illinois
SECRETARY OF THE SOCIETY

THE SUBJECT OF THIS YEARBOOK WILL BE DISCUSSED AT THE WASHINGTON MEETINGS OF THE NATIONAL SOCIETY ON MONDAY, FEBRUARY 24, AT 7:45 P. M., AND WEDNESDAY, FEBRUARY 26, 1908, AT 4:30 P. M.

CHICAGO
THE UNIVERSITY OF CHICAGO PRESS
1908

GENERAL

Composed and Printed By
The University of Chicago Press
Chicago, Illinois, U. S. A.

OFFICERS AND EXECUTIVE COMMITTEE

STRATTON D. BROOKS,
Superintendent of Schools, Boston, Mass.
President

REUBEN POST HALLECK,
Boys' High School, Louisville, Ky.

W. S. SUTTON,
University of Texas, Austin, Texas

J. STANLEY BROWN,
Superintendent Township High School, Joliet, Ill.

HENRY SUZZALLO,
Teachers College, Columbia University, New York

MANFRED J. HOLMES,
Illinois State Normal University, Normal, Ill.
Secretary-Treasurer
and
Editor of Yearbook

TABLE OF CONTENTS

PREFACE

Three years ago the subject of the *Seventh Yearbook* was proposed as an important field for the National Society to investigate. Since that time several of the ablest and most progressive superintendents in the United States have made positive advance in the solution of the problems involved in the relation of superintendents and principals to the training and improvement of their teachers.

That the study presented in this *Yearbook* should have been made by one who has been connected with the movement at perhaps its most active storm center is fortunate for manifest reasons. Charles D. Lowry has been a district superintendent of schools in Chicago for about seven years, and therefore has the insight necessary to interpret the reports sent in from all parts of the United States and select and classify and estimate the value of data contained in such reports.

It is hoped that this *Yearbook* will be of service to superintendents, principals, and boards of education who are earnestly working to solve the important and difficult problem involved.

One important part of the *Seventh Yearbook* is intentionally postponed to be published later under separate cover. This part omitted is the supplementary study of the kindergarten in its relation to elementary education. This supplement is to be devoted entirely to the practical relation, the necessary unity and continuity of kindergarten and primary education. Subscribers to the *Yearbook* will get this supplement as a part of the present issue without extra charge.

M. J. HOLMES

INTRODUCTION

Recently there was sent out by the secretary of this Society to many of its members and others, a circular[1] asking each (1) to give his views as to the need for carrying on systematic work for training the teaching force to a higher degree of efficiency, and (2) to make a statement of the nature of such work, if any, that is carried on in the school system with which he is connected. A number of very interesting replies were received. The following paper is practically a summary of these reports. No effort has

[1] This circular read as follows:

The next meeting of the Society for the Scientific Study of Education (February, 1908) will be devoted to the discussion of the relation of superintendents and principals to the improvement of teachers after they have entered the profession. To Mr. C. D. Lowry, district superintendent, Chicago, has been assigned the duty of preparing the paper. This paper is to contain (1) a statement of the reasons why the work of improvement of teachers should be carried on systematically, and (2) a summary of the best methods that are in use throughout the country to attain the end desired.

Will you kindly prepare a statement covering these two points as seen from the standpoint of the work in your city? The inclosed questionnaire has been prepared simply to make your reply easier. It need not be followed if you prefer to adopt some other plan.

It will be particularly interesting to know what is being done in your city for the improvement of teachers. Wherever printed rules of the board of education will supply this information, kindly furnish a copy.

This paper will be printed in the *Yearbook* of the Society. We hope to make it a valuable handbook for superintendents and boards of education. It is therefore desirable that the information be as full and accurate as possible. We should also like the privilege of printing *verbatim* portions of any returns that may seem suited for such use.

The importance of this study and its practical value when published in book form surely warrant our asking even the busiest superintendents to co-operate by returning at the earliest possible day the data herein requested.

The time for preparing the paper is short; therefore please send reply directly to C. D. Lowry, district superintendent, Board of Education Rooms, Chicago, Ill.

Yours very respectfully,

MANFRED J. HOLMES,
Secretary, and Editor of YEARBOOK

been made to state the number of replies to each point nor the number of places reporting a certain kind of work, the effort being to present, as a whole, the views of the various correspondents on the question of the need for the work and a summary of the leading lines of work that are being undertaken. In a few instances, the rules of the boards of education have been quoted or summarized.

The thanks of the writer are hereby extended to all who so kindly co-operated in this work. The author has added but little to the statements found in the various papers.

Two important lines of work for the improvement of teachers have not been touched in this study, namely, the "Preparation of Teachers," and the "Certification of Teachers." Both of these topics, however, have been treated in previous Yearbooks of the Society.

THE RELATION OF PRINCIPALS AND SUPERINTENDENTS TO THE TRAINING AND IMPROVEMENT OF THEIR TEACHERS

CHARLES D. LOWRY
District Superintendent of Schools, Chicago, Ill.

THE PROBLEM

Success in any occupation depends upon the native ability, the initial equipment, and the intensity of the desire for improvement existing in the worker. This statement applies to work in its broadest sense, including that of the artist, the professional man, and the mechanic.

The intensity of the desire for improvement is in direct proportion to the stimulus which it receives. This stimulus may come from the worker's conscientiousness and his love for excellence, or it may be the result of external influences, such as the opportunity to obtain pecuniary or other rewards. Conscientiousness and love for excellence are peculiar to no rank of society; there will be, doubtless, about as many people having these qualities in one occupation as in another. The effect of this stimulus, therefore, is about equally potent in all. The differences lie chiefly in the external stimulation.

In most occupations the encouragement for improvement is furnished by the conditions governing the practice of the occupation itself. A physician who is not well equipped, who is unsuccessful in diagnosis, who does not keep abreast of progress in the treatment of disease, cannot retain any considerable practice and is seldom trusted with difficult cases. The public knowing little of medicine, can yet apply the rule of judging a tree by its fruits; they can tell a sick child from a well one and they soon learn to judge pretty fairly as to a physician's ability to heal.

With the teaching profession, it is otherwise. The public are not so successful in discriminating a well-taught child from one poorly taught. The indications are not so pronounced. The sick child is unhappy and makes those about him suffer; the poorly taught child is not unhappy and seldom causes his parents much anxiety on that score; the mischief is insidious; the consequences come to the surface only in later years.

In medicine the public demands that which is modern. In school work, they are apt to demand the ancient. Parents like to have their children taught in the good old-fashioned way. The desire for better work does not come from the public, but from the progressive members of the teaching profession. This, then, is the first and greatest reason why the present topic, "The Relation of the Principal and the Superintendent to the Improvement of Teachers," is of special importance. The plans for improvement must originate with them and be carried forward by them, if they are ever to come at all.

When the conditions under which the work of teaching is done are examined into, the need for carrying this work on steadily and systematically is shown more clearly. To carry a little farther the comparison between the medical profession and that of teaching: the physician cannot begin to practice until he has passed through a lengthy and somewhat severe course of training, which training has been passed upon by legally constituted authorities. This severe requirement is of recent growth. A century ago, a man might begin the practice of medicine with as much ease and as little training as is needed today in many parts of the country for young men and young women to begin teaching. The laws in force in many of the larger cities give great encouragement to teachers who have graduated from accredited normal schools having at least a two-year course, and to students who have graduated from accredited colleges having pedagogical courses; but it is still true that owing to the scarcity of teachers there are being admitted to the service in practically all school systems teachers who began their work with only a high-school education, and in many places with much less than this. Furthermore, there are today in probably all school systems many teachers who began their service before the requirements were anything like as high as they are today, and when the examinations themselves were much easier than they are now. Therefore, without relaxing their efforts to secure a high degree of preparation in teachers, the superintendent and the principal must give more time and attention to making good teachers of those now in service.

The situation is well illustrated by the following quotations:

In Baltimore for many years prior to 1900, the indispensable minimum of scholarship for teaching in the elementary schools was provided for by the requirement of high-school graduation or its equivalent as a condition of employment. Graduation from the high school was here, as in many other cities, very ill-advisedly taken as evidence of ability to teach. A few years earlier, a still lower standard prevailed. There are teachers yet in the service whose attainments at the time of their appointment were tested only by an examination about suited to pupils in an upper grammar grade of an elementary school. These, however, are few, and they have gained increased scholarship while teaching. In either case the young teacher was placed in charge of a class with only the empirical ideas about teaching that came unconsciously from years of association in elementary and high schools with her own teachers, themselves, in many instances, not especially well qualified for their work, and consequently, presenting for imitation not the best models. A teacher thus equipped has some knowledge of the common branches, but she knows little of the learning process and, therefore, her efforts are uneconomically expended. She does not know how to present subjects in such a manner as to engage the child's interest and call forth his best efforts; consequently, disciplinary problems are the prominent ones. She begins with the younger children because these are the only ones she can keep in order. A few teachers of superior natural ability quickly gain considerable skill; others, in the course of time, achieve a moderate degree of success; and still others, equally conscientious and faithful, begin their work in a purely formal and mechanical way, and, if left undisturbed, soon become chained in a dull and lifeless routine.

The situation as regards the teaching force of Kansas City (Mo.) is similar to that of many other cities rapidly growing. The demand for teachers is constant. We employ as many experienced teachers from the outside as are attracted to us by the salary offered. Previous to 1891, eligibility to appointment to the city schools depended upon passing an examination given by the county commissioner. Few applicants ever failed to pass it. Teachers, except those holding state certificates, were examined annually or biennially, therefore, for the purpose of keeping up the standard(?). Attendance at the county institute was recognized as an equivalent. Few ever were absent. About 1891, the state legislature changed the law relating to the examination of our city teachers. Since that time a committee of two principals and a high-school teacher has constituted the examining board, the standard of whose examinations has been essentially higher than that of the county commissioner.

The school board of Kansas City does not require professional training. As conditions are now it could not make such a requirement. We have no city training school, no city normal .college, no teachers' college. Of the annual output of the five normal schools in the state, we receive, obviously, a very small part. Neither is conformity to a high standard of scholarship required, unless the ability to pass the preliminary examination is so accounted. While the school board places a correct value on a college diploma, it is not required. Notwithstanding this, a considerable number of the teachers, both in the high schools and in the elementary schools, are college bred. . . . . We have among us scholarly teachers who are graduates of high schools only. Their student days have never ended. We have among us representatives of both foreign and American universities. We have teachers of native ability who have had but little, if any, strictly professional preparation. We have teachers who, to a general education, have added such professional training as is given in a two-year course at a state normal school, and others who have taken a year's course. Among our teachers are several who, previous to accepting an appointment in this city, were teaching in a normal school, or a college, or acting as superintendent of a town-school system. We have representatives from several teachers' colleges. We also have teachers who were educated in various academies such as once flourished in many of the states. And we have the contingent, increasing each year, that has graduated from the city high schools, passed the teachers' examination, substituted one year in the schools, and received temporary appointment as teachers. During the period of substituting, these beginners have learned a few devices. They are almost helpless if left to themselves. They have little knowledge of children and little knowledge of the subjects to be taught. They belong to no school of thought, they know nothing of the philosophy of education, or of its history, or of its principles, or of its practice. These at a small salary are put in charge of a room. They have youth and personal charm, and what may be called flexibility of character; they are enthusiastic and eager to succeed. Their personality tides them over the period of their novitiate, and if they remain in the service, they sometimes become valuable members of it.

To quote from the report from Grand Rapids (Wis.):

After such a teacher (high-school graduate) has had a little experience she acquires considerable mechanical skill in teaching. Professional knowledge is liable to become limited to methods and devices. Theories underlying the devices and the larger problems of the nature of the child become to her a sealed book which she neither knows how to open nor does she consider it worth her while to make an attempt.

Even when the teachers who enter the service come with the preparation furnished by the best normal schools and colleges, there is still need for much careful training and instruction. The college graduate while well equipped from an academic standpoint, has only theoretical knowledge of methods of presenting material and of the training and management of children. It is a common experience that these teachers are apt to make a failure in the class-room at the beginning of their work unless they are carefully supported and directed until they have acquired, from practice, skill in meeting classroom problems. With the normal-school graduate, no matter how well the practice work done in connection with her training has been arranged, there must be something artificial about it and the conditions that confront the teacher when she is thrown entirely upon her own resources are very different from those to which she has been accustomed. On the other hand, much of the instruction which she has received on the theoretical lines has been but partly comprehended since she had no real body of experience with which to interpret it; hence, much of the greatest value will have been forgotten before the opportunity to apply has come, and its value in helping her to solve her problems of school work will be largely lost unless it is recalled to her through continued study and careful supervision, and unless the applications of these doctrines of education are pointed out to her in practice. Moreover, these young women rush from childish studies to professional discipline and without having really passed through the changes of girlhood, they undertake to shape the plastic minds of children, minds from which they have by their own rapid physical and emotional growth been removed farther in sympathy than are men and women of more mature years.

A few years ago, the complaint was frequent that the insecurity of tenure worked against the attaining of the best service in the school work. This complaint still applies, no doubt, in rural communities and smaller cities. In the larger cities, the condition is quite the reverse. After a teacher has once become established in a system by virtue of one or two years of moderately successful work, her position becomes practically permanent if she continues to do work which is barely mediocre; and the adoption, in many places, of laws, establishing a teachers' pension fund, by giving the teachers a sort of legal claim to their positions, has also given much comfort to the mediocre teacher.

Still another, and, perhaps, the most serious reason why it is important to train teachers to their highest efficiency is this: in practically every occupation but ours when a worker becomes less and less efficient, and where, for any reason, it is desirable to retain him in the service, there are found positions of less and less importance which he can fill acceptably or with little detriment to the service. In a graded school, on the contrary, the teacher of the highest efficiency and the teacher of less efficiency have equally important problems to solve, and poor work by either is equally harmful. Each teacher is in charge of forty or fifty children for five hours a day during the years when the physical, mental, and spiritual natures of those children are most plastic. If there is any difference in this regard, it is that the poorer teachers are placed in the lower grades where their weakness is less apparent—the places of all others the worst for the poor teacher, her apparent success in these grades being due to her ability to form these immature and plastic minds upon the bad ideals which she herself represents.

THE SOLUTION

The lines of work reported may be roughly divided into five classes: (1) supervision; (2) work undertaken voluntarily by teachers; (3) work required of teachers; (4) work stimulated by pecuniary rewards or advance in position; (5) miscellaneous.

These lines of work are not always distinct from each other; for example, the work undertaken voluntarily is often that suggested by the superintendent and oftentimes, no doubt, suggested so directly as to seem almost a requirement.

I. *Supervision*

The first method for the improvement of teachers, and the one in most general use, is that of supervision in its various forms. In the smaller cities, the teacher has a peculiar advantage because she is under the supervision of a principal, who has under him but a few teachers, and also the supervision of a superintendent, whose entire corps may be less than one hundred, so that every teacher is known intimately by both the principal and the superintendent and the needs of each one may be carefully discussed and promptly met. In many of the smaller cities, in addition to the regular teachers there are special teachers of music, drawing, manual training, physical training. These teachers either conduct the work in their respective departments themselves or supervise the work as done by the regular teacher. Where the latter course is pursued, the special teacher gives model lessons in each of the class-rooms, criticizes the work that has been done since the last visit, gives directions for future work, and holds classes or institutes for the instruction of teachers in these branches. In many cities the entire work in these special subjects is under the care of the special teachers and the individual principals have little responsibility in the matter.

In a few cities supervision is further extended. In Baltimore, for example, grade supervisors devote their attention to the super-vision of the work in one or two grades, the advantage being that by having supervision of such a narrow range of work the super-visor becomes very expert, and the work in all of the schools is brought up to the standard of the excellence of the supervisor her-self as far as that is consistent with the varying ability of the teachers with whom she works. She has the advantage of compar-ing the work done in her special grades in the various schools in the city—an advantage which the principal confined to one building cannot have.

In other places, the work is still further subdivided by the appointment of supervisors of a single subject, as, for instance, arithmetic, throughout the primary grades. A very interesting form of supervision is that given by the supervisor of substitutes, which is reported from one or two cities. This teacher visits each teacher as she begins her work, helps her in the preparation of out-lines and in the various problems that arise, meets the entire body of substitutes at stated intervals for purposes of study and instruc-tion. She also visits the newly appointed teacher, works with her in the classroom for a day at a time, and then sends her to visit some other classroom while the supervisor takes charge of the work. On the third day, she remains with the new teacher, discusses with her the conditions that have arisen in her absence and the work which she has seen in the school which she visited.

A most interesting work for associations of schools in rural communities is that undertaken by Superintendent Cook, in Baltimore County (Md.). Here a supervisor has been appointed to visit and instruct teachers in the work of the primary grades, and another to instruct them in the work in the grammar grades. The supervisor meets each group of teachers once a month and small groups are organized for the consideration of special studies on Saturdays or in the evenings. The board of education contributes toward the expense of these classes.

Beyond question this work of supervision is and always will be the most important of all the ways in which the character of the teaching is to be improved. As the superintendent is, so is the force, especially in the smaller cities where the personality of the superintendent. can be felt through all the parts of the system. This influence is exerted in many ways. Mr. Gay, of Haverhill, says:

In visits for personal inspection and suggestion, I am generous in praise of the good things which I see, and criticise only when I believe my criticism will be received in the right spirit and will probably work improvement. I gave up years ago all criticism for the sake of freeing myself from responsibility. Often I refrain from direct criticism and talk to the principal of the school concerning the teacher's faults. I am reaching the conclusion that I would better always consult the principal before making criticism of any kind. The reason for this will be appreciated by every experienced superintendent.

The best method of helping teachers is, I believe, by example. The superintendent or principal should be always at his post of duty, and always within call of every teacher to assist her in any possible way. Early and late, in season and out of season, school days and holidays, it should be known that he is trying to do all that his time and strength will permit to promote the interests of the schools. He must always say "Come;" must study harder and work more hours than his teachers; must set a pace which his best teachers find it impossible to follow. Otherwise, he should resign and let some one who will do more and better work take his place.

Mr. Arthur Le Fevre, of Victoria, Tex., gives some good theoretical views regarding the work of the superintendent.

His work with teachers should be toward forming right ideals as to education, the training of enlightened, steadfast character, the developing of power, of inner freedom, of courage; to point out to teachers the futility of conning textbooks prepared for young pupils and to supply a list of books belonging to the real literature of each branch of study. If a teacher of any subject has read in it only children's schoolbooks, an almost incredible sense of power and of widened horizon would result from the perusal of a book opening an insight into the true perspective of that field of human achievement and present effort. What has been dark or trivial and empty, would forthwith become for the teacher and pupil full of bright and stimulating interest.

He should train teachers, principals, and supervisors into a spirit of sincere co-operation. Each member of the force should be made to feel a responsibility for a high standard of accomplishment in his department, and also for the work of the whole system. Each member of the force should be free in minor details in executing the work assigned.

It should be the constant care of the superintendent to make the conditions under which the work of teaching is done as favorable as possible.

Next in importance to the supervision of the superintendent comes that of the principal. Indeed, in our larger cities, his supervision, as far as it touches the work of the individual teacher, is by far the more important. He is often in charge of more pupils than are found in the entire school population of a moderate-size town. The work of a given school in one of our cosmopolitan cities may be strikingly different from that of its neighbors. One school may be made up of Jewish children, an adjoining one of Italian, and a third, of Swedish. In one school in Chicago there are pupils representing nearly every prominent race of Europe and many of the smaller ones. Each school must adapt itself to the needs of its community. This work must have a unity and no one can unify it but the principal; his office should be magnified, his responsibility increased. The policy of instruction, whether in the regular or in the special subjects, should be his and not that of the visiting supervisor, no matter how expert she may be in her particular line. Expert assistance he, of course, needs; but as far as is possible, this should come from teachers located permanently in the school. Every school faculty should contain such expert talent. If the importance of this policy is appreciated and a consistent effort is made to bring about the result just mentioned, it will be surprising to find out how much latent talent there exists in every school corps —talent which may be wonderfully developed by careful training. This development is difficult if a teacher is placed in charge of a single room for an entire year and expected to teach all the subjects in the curriculum. But even if this plan is pursued, the principal, by carefully noticing the special aptitudes of his teachers, can utilize the special skill of each to instruct the others, and thus, in a measure, give to each teacher in his school the benefit of the help of the best work of all. This policy not only will have a helpful initial influence upon the work of the school, but the effect is cumulative. Every one likes to be appreciated and if a teacher feels that her special talent is recognized, she will labor earnestly to improve herself still further in this direction. A secondary and very vital gain will result from the spirit of friendliness and mutual helpfulness developed in the school. This will be of great value. The united efforts of twenty-five people are of immensely more influence than the separate efforts of the same number.

Another, and still better way to make use of the talents of the various teachers is by means of the so-called departmental plan of instruction. This method, by relieving teachers from the necessity of preparing their work in a great variety of subjects and thus allowing them the opportunity, time, and strength for special preparation in favorite lines, tends to produce a corps of scholarly, expert teachers from one that was previously only of the ordinary grade. This policy has been pursued in many of the schools of Chicago. In one school, where the departmental method is used, the entire work in the ordinary subjects and also in singing, drawing, manual training, and domestic science is carried on by the regular grade teachers. It is surely better to work toward this end than to distract the teacher by requiring her allegiance to supervisors of separate grades, of arithmetic, drawing, sewing, construction work, physical training, etc.

The plan of making the school a unit is of equal and, perhaps, greater importance in the training it gives to the principal. When the principal is relieved of responsibility in the special subjects, he loses interest in them, and these subjects not only suffer from lack of the daily supervision which can be given only by the principal who is present at all times, but they lose by becoming isolated from the other school work. Thus results a lack of unity in the school experience of the children, which is oftentimes detrimental. In Chicago, while there are still special teachers, responsibility has of late years been placed more and more in the hands of the principal of the school. He is made to feel that the success of the work in drawing, for example, depends as much upon his interest and skill as does the success of the work in the ordinary subjects, such as mathematics or history.

A visiting supervisor should work through the principal, advising with him rather than with the teachers direct. In no case should the supervisor issue orders to the teacher. It should be her business to point out to the principal the needs of the various teachers; to give assistance to these teachers in ways which the principal may decide. This process, while indirect, and hence slow, tends to place responsibility and hence, ultimately, to produce a high degree of efficiency.

From the admirable report of Mr. Van Sickle is quoted the following classification of teachers and statement of the duties of the supervising force in relation to each class:

(1) Superior teachers who need no stimulation other than their own ideals of excellence: By the fine standard of work which they maintain and by their student-like habits they might under favorable conditions, set the pace for the entire teaching force. At the present time, this group is a large one. With this group, supervision is chiefly concerned in gaining their co-operation in working out the problems and in bringing their influences to bear on other teachers in tactful ways.

(2) Teachers possessing a good degree of executive ability and adequate scholarship of the book-learning variety, who resist change because they honestly believe the old ways are better: They are patriotic defenders of the views and traditions and practices in which they were reared. The greater number of these will as strongly support the new when fully convinced of its advantages; but in the absence of positive orders they resist proposed changes until absolutely conclusive demonstration is furnished in a concrete way. Supervision must confidently accept these conditions and furnish demonstration.

(3) Teachers lacking adequate scholarship or practical skill or both, self-conscious and timid, because unacquainted with standards of work and valid guiding principles, desirous of avoiding observation, doing their work in a more or less perfunctory and fortuitous way: supervision needs to give these teachers courage by an exhibition of standards plainly within their reach and by personal work in their own classrooms.

(4) Teachers lacking adequate scholarship or practical skill or both, but not conscious of this lack and therefore unaware of any need of assistance:

Some form of positive direction is here necessary in the first stages of supervision.

(5) Teachers yet in the early years of their service: Supervision should be able to concern itself chiefly in keeping these teachers in class 1 so far as their personal attitude is concerned. There will, of course, always be differcuces among them in scholarship and personal power, but all should have guidance in kind and quantity adapted to prevent any of them, even the weakest, from developing the characteristics of class 2, class 3, or class 4. If these new recruits are to be able to lead children to be open-minded, to hold opinions tentatively, to be sure but not too sure, to be willing to give both sides of a question a hearing before reaching a final conclusion, they must keep themselves open-minded. To aid them in doing this, supervision will keep itself free from dogmatism even in dealing with the youngest teachers.

Teachers of class 1, class 2, and class 5 are willing to have their work seen and valued by competent and trusted supervisors. People who know how to do a thing, or who sincerely think they know how, or who sincerely wish to learn how, are neither afraid nor reluctant to have their work seen by any fair-minded person. Supervisors must be both skilful and fair-minded, and their work must prove that supervision means help.

II· *Voluntary Work*

The second form of work is that undertaken by the teachers themselves either individually or through organizations encouraged by school authorities. This work is very extensive. It is reported from every city from which replies have been received. This is a high tribute to the enthusiasm and devotion of teachers to their work. It takes the form of work in colleges or in normal-school classes, university extension, normal-school extension, book reviews, neighborhood clubs for the study of various subjects, and lecture associations. Providence, Rhode Island, reports that, as a result of an inquiry made some years ago, it was found that of thirty-three high-school men, twenty-three had, while teaching, taken distinct courses at various colleges and several had studied abroad; of forty-four high-school women, thirty-one had done similar work in colleges or elsewhere; eight men had received A.M.'s or Ph.D.'s. These degrees had been given for work accomplished; they were not honorary. Many certificates had been received from Harvard, Clark, and the University of Chicago for summer work; of forty-five kindergartners, forty had pursued studies along the line of their work, while others had taken work in general culture at Brown University; of 464 grade teachers, 313 had carried on studies of various kinds. During the past winter, several hundred took the Brown University extension course; fifty-six took examinations and received credits toward degrees.

Decatur (Ill.) reported that 90 per cent. of the grade teachers attended summer schools.

One of the most interesting of these voluntary organizations is reported from Kansas City (Mo.). In 1878, Superintendent J. M. Greenwood and a few friends formed a coterie for the study of the modern philosophical systems. Ten years later the scope of topics was widened. These years had been devoted to the study of philosophical systems, literary phases of the world, and economic conditions of the different countries.

The club, now called the "Greenwood Club," is composed of such citizens as are disposed favorably toward a higher and broader education, including teachers, preachers, doctors, lawyers, and business men. The plan of work is simple. There is no formality. A president and a treasurer are the only officers. Subjects are assigned by a committee. A paper from thirty to forty minutes in length is presented by an essayist. After the paper, the subject is before the club and any one present may participate in the discussion.

The general influence of this organization upon the teaching force of the city has been remarkable. Every strong teacher who has been selected to take positions elsewhere on account of superior qualifications has been an active member of this club. The primary object had in view was to give breadth and a wider scope to the general scholarship of the teachers of the city. The topics discussed during the long series of years of the club's existence have been of the highest order and extend over practically the whole range of human interest. A few will show the character: Gaul under Roman Influence; The Rise of Modern Thought; Victor Hugo and His Contemporaries (a long series of meetings) ; The Early History of Kansas City; The Gospel for the Modern Day Congregation; The Club a Menace to the Home; The Standpoint of the Parent; Municipal Ownership; Recent Progress in Therapeutics.

The solid effects of such a club can scarcely be overestimated. It brings the teacher into contact with the thinking men and women of other walks of life, and in this way she loses the narrowness and somewhat unpractical cast of thought which is a frequent consequence of long associations with immature minds.

A very valuable work reported from several cities is that of a systematic consideration by committees of principals or teachers of the various topics in the course of study or of various phases of teaching. In Chicago for several years, the principals of the schools were divided up into committees for the study of the regular subjects in the course of study. Each committee began by formulating a tentative plan of subject-matter, materials, and methods of teaching. The details of these plans, especially those portions about which there was a difference of opinion, were then taken up by each principal and discussed with his teachers and tested in actual schoolroom practice. The results of this work in the school were then reported back to the committee and a new formulation was undertaken and new phases of the work taken up. This course was systematically pursued through a long period; the outcome being a series of monographs on the topics of the course of study. These again were utilized in the formation of a tentative course of study. This course was put in practice for one year; at the end of the year reports were received from each school, and a new course formulated. This was again put in practice for a year, and a second series of reports called for. The formulation of this course of study as a result of the latter reports has just been completed though it is considered that the course is by no means fixed. The result of this continuous study into the values and methods used in the schools not only resulted in greatly improving the nature of the material and the methods but also had an extremely helpful influence upon the principals and teachers themselves.

The following very interesting lines of work are reported from St. Louis (Mo.):

First of these should be named the Society of Pedagogy, a purely voluntary organization whose annual membership reaches about fifteen hundred, of which at least twelve hundred are teachers in the St. Louis Public Schools. The section meetings assemble on the first and third Saturday mornings of each month, October to April. The society also maintains a course of lectures during the season, presenting usually eight or ten notable people each season. Some of the topics discussed are the following: pedagogy; educational psychology; current school topics; the Renaissance; physiography; French; Spanish; manual training; classics; Shakespeare; contemporary literature; United States history; primary geography; singing; physics.

The next notable opportunity presented is in the classes of the Saturday Normal College. These classes are held on the second and fourth Saturday mornings of each month, October to April, and are designed primarily for the apprentice teachers, who are required to attend. They are held in the Critique Room of the Teachers' College, which will permit an audience of about three hundred and is usually filled to its utmost capacity by the voluntary attendance of teachers whose grade work is being illustrated, these classes being always in the nature of practical illustrations.

A third and extremely important opportunity is that furnished by the extension course of the Teachers' College. It is a notable fact that these classes are always filled to their extreme limit.

Length of course: Courses will continue for twenty weeks beginning at the Teachers' College, October 8, and at the Sumner High School, October 9, and closing March, 1908.

Recitation periods: Classes in all subjects will meet once each week at 4:15 P. M. and continue in session one hour.

Regulation as to enrollment and attendance: It is requested that teachers enroll in one course only. No teacher will be allowed to enroll in more than two courses.

Owing to laboratory conditions, the class in biology, will be limited to twenty-four members. It is intended that members in all other classes, except the chorus class, shall not exceed thirty. No class will be organized with less than fifteen members, and any class will be discontinued whose number in attendance for three consecutive weeks falls below ten.

Not more than four nor less than two hours of home study each week will be necessary.

Nature of instruction: Each subject will be presented, as far as possible, from both the academical and pedagogical points of view, and the fullest opportunity will be given for the intellectual activity and growth of each individual student.

III. *Required Work*

To begin with the country teachers: In many counties they are required to attend during the summer an institute of from five to ten days of from five to seven hours each; if the work of these periods involved a series of lines of systematic work, it would be equivalent to carrying one or two courses in college through a year. In addition, they are required during the year, to read two books;

one on a professional subject and one on an academic subject. Oftentimes they are expected to make written reports upon these books or to pass examinations upon them. In a few communities, the teachers are expected to attend summer schools, of from two to four weeks each.

In quite a number of the states the certificate to teach is valid for only a short time—from six months to three years; thus making it necessary for the teacher to pass new examinations at brief intervals. In most of the cities, the candidate's first certificate is valid for one year, but is renewed at the end of the first year if the work has been satisfactory. The certificate is again renewed under the same conditions at the end of the second year and if at the end of the third year the work is still satisfactory, the certificate becomes permanent. During these years of probation, the character of the work is reported upon by the various supervisors, by the principals or superintendents who have observed the work; and, in some instances, where there are special classes for beginners, the completion of certain work in these beginners' classes is taken into account in determining the standing of the young teacher.

For the great body of teachers in cities, the required work takes the form of institutes or study classes; of these, there are a great variety. In Kansas City (Mo.) we find the following:

1. The institute: A regular monthly meeting on Saturdays, from nine to twelve o'clock, organized in three divisions: The Primary Section, the Grammar Section, and the High-School Section. It includes all principals and teachers in the public schools. The first half hour is devoted to the general meeting in charge of the superintendent. From 9:30 to 11, the institute is divided into a number of groups in each of which there is carried on a connected line of study. A few of the topics selected from recent programs indicate the character of the work. Elementary Grade Section: Primitive German Life and Character; Teaching of Spelling, Grammar, Geography, etc. High-School Section: Manual Training, Its Physiological Value, Its Industrial Value, Its Ethical Value; Sociological Problems of Kansas City; Shortcomings of the High-School English Course. At 11 o'clock, the general program is presented, the main feature of which is a formal address by some person of note.

2. The monthly consultation of principals with their teachers on the last Friday of each school month, meeting of one hour: This hour is devoted either to conferences on school management or to intensive study along some one line. In one school, the meetings each year for a series of years, were devoted to the study of some particular topic in literature, a few of which were—Talks on the Study of Literature; Freytag's *Technique of the Drama;* Horne's *Philosophy of Education.*

3. Monthly principal's meeting, from 9 to 12 on Saturdays: The final object of which is to get the best experience from all of the principals and to serve as a means for propagating in the field of education the dominant educational ideas of the world.

The high order of the work done in these meetings is indicated by topics selected from a recent program: Importance of Diplomatic History; The Janitor's Side of the Public School Work; The Scientific and Scholastic Training of the Educators in Germany is the Cause of German Industrial and Commercial Supremacy; A Comparison of the Educational Systems of France and Japan; The Elementary and Secondary Schools of England Compared with the Elementary and Secondary Schools of Missouri.

Papers on these subjects were presented by two principals at each of the meetings. Many cities report a similar series of meetings.

In addition to these, many cities report institutes, which the teachers are required to attend, held by the special teachers of physical training, of drawing, and of music. Also, grade institutes, and institutes in particular subjects as, grammar, history, etc., are held at frequent intervals, especially at the beginning of the year. In the smaller cities, these meetings are presided over by the superintendent of schools. Here all the teachers of a grade are gathered together and some topic is discussed and some work is taken up that is of common interest, or the best methods of teaching subjects of the grades in question are presented by means of model lessons given by teachers who are particularly expert.

In certain small cities, the superintendent conducts a class in professional study meeting once a week for one hour; all teachers are expected to attend this class.

One of the most interesting organizations is the Helena Kindergarten Council which has been in existence for a number of years. It is composed of the teachers of the kindergarten and of the early primary grades. It holds eight meetings a year devoted to a great variety of topics connected with the work of the grades in question. Some of these taken from different programs are as follows: The Child in Action (three meetings); The Intellectual Development of the Child; Kindergarten Out-of-Doors; The Kindergarten and the Primary Grades; The Value of the Positive rather than the Negative in Work; The Kindergarten in Many Lines (topics for an entire year).

The amount that is thus required of a teacher in a year's attendance upon these classes is quite large, certainly in most cases equivalent to two hours a week. In many cases, it is undoubtedly larger. This is not an undue requirement, and if profitably employed must result in great good to the work of the teacher.

IV. *Work Stimulated by Advance in Salary or in Rank*

The teacher, besides endeavoring to improve in directions that are pointed out to her by those with whom she works, must herself be an independent student. This is necessary in order that her intellectual horizon shall be constantly broadening and that her mind be kept pliable and in that state of efficiency designated in the field of athletics as "in training," for in no other way will she be able to grasp the problems that are constantly arising in this, the most complex of professions, and in no other way can she retain her sympathy with the learning minds over which she has care and her ability to direct these minds. Again, teaching, while it is a very conservative profession, is yet rapidly changing both as to methods and as to subject-matter. The teacher who was well equipped ten years ago is now hopelessly out of date unless she has been constantly advancing with the changes in method and in curriculum. Without regular vigorous study, the mind loses its ability to grasp the spirit of these great changes.

Miss Gertrude Edmund of Lowell, Mass., reports:

I know many teachers who are and have been pursuing professional and collegiate courses of study in connection with their regular school work, and in every case which has come under my observation these men and women have been and are today better teachers for having continued their studies.

They are sympathetic in their attitude toward the efforts of the young teachers and pupils; their minds are not decreasing in strength and mental alertness, but are open to receive new truths, and they are willing to embody these truths in practical lines of work.

The previous pages give abundant evidence that many teachers are willing to do this studying with no other motive than the love of learning and the satisfaction of being a master in one's chosen calling. This work is its own best reward, but since it is of value to the schools, it is reasonable that it should be rewarded in a tangible way, by increased salaries and by promotions. Moreover, this external motive will appeal to many who are not moved by the internal stimulus, and these are the ones who, for the good of the service, are most in need of uplifting. In endeavoring to apply this principle several cities have introduced plans which make advancement in rank or in salary depend (1) on excellence of work; (2) on presentation of evidence of some form of self-directed study.

Of the plans which give chief prominence to opportunities for promotion in rank, that of New York City is the most elaborate. This plan provides for a system of licenses which are granted partly upon record of successful service, partly upon examinations in scholarship in academic and professional subjects, and partly upon presentation of certificates showing the completion of courses in academic subjects, in colleges or universities of approved standing. The entire system will be best understood from the report of Dr. Maxwell:

"*License No. 1* is granted to candidates upon passing a professional examination in the history and principles of education, and methods of teaching, an examination in academic subjects, an oral examination to enable the examiner to estimate the applicant's use of English and general personal fitness, and a physical examination. The candidate is exempted from the academic examination upon presentation of credentials showing such work as is the equivalent to the ordinary college-entrance requirements."

There are also certain requirements as to experience in teaching.

Higher licenses are granted upon work done at a grade above that required for License No. 1. They are as follows:

Promotion Licenses.—The following are the provisions of the by-laws of the Board of Education relative to a license for promotion:

A license for promotion shall qualify the holder to act as teacher in the grades of the last two years of the elementary-school course, but no person not now teaching in the last two years of the elementary-school course shall be appointed teacher of a graduating class, who, in addition to the holding of the license for promotion, has not served at least two years in other grades of the last two years of the course.

This license shall qualify the holder to act as assistant teacher in an evening high school.

To be eligible for license for promotion to any grade in the last two years of the elementary-school course, applicants must have the following qualifications:

a) The holding of License No. 1.

b) Successful experience in teaching, as determined by records and reports of superintendents and principals, equivalent to three years' experience in the public schools of the city of New York, including one year's experience in the city of New York.

c) Examination in the principles and methods of teaching, or, in lieu of such examination, the completion in an approved institution of satisfactory courses amounting to at least sixty hours in principles and methods of teaching; and examination in one of the following subjects or groups of subjects as prescribed in the course of study for elementary schools: English (reading, grammar, composition); mathematics (arithmetic, elementary algebra, elementary geometry); history (United States history and civics); geography and elementary science; constructive work and drawing; such other subjects or groups of subjects in the course of study as may be specified by the Board of Superintendents.'

Exemption is granted from examination in the principles and methods of teaching to those who complete in an approved institution satisfactory courses amounting to at least sixty hours in principles and methods of teaching.

NOTES.—(*a*) No exemption for the license is granted from examination in the required academic subjects or groups of subjects, viz., English, mathematics, history, geography, and science, constructive work and drawing, etc.

b) No exemption is granted for studies not included under "principles and methods of teaching." For purposes of exemption under this head "principles and methods of teaching" will be regarded as including science of education, history of education, psychology (educational, applied, genetic, pure), general method, methods of teaching special subjects, school management.

c) No course will be accepted which was not pursued in a college, university, or extension center recognized by the Regents of the University of the State of New York.

d) No course of less than thirty hours' attendance is accepted.

e) No course is accepted that was not terminated by a successful examination.

f) Exemption is granted only for courses in excess of the studies which were required to establish the eligibility of the applicant for License No. 1.

Assistant to Principal.—The by-laws provide as follows:

A license as assistant to principal or head of department shall qualify the holder for the position of assistant to principal in an elementary school or of principal of an evening elementary school or of a vacation school, or to act as teacher in charge of an elementary school of the fourth order.

To be eligible for license as assistant to principal in elementary schools, the applicant must have the following qualifications:

a) The holding of a permanent License No. 1, and not less than eight years' successful experience in teaching or supervision in the schools of the city of New York, or experience rated as equivalent thereto.

b) A license as principal in elementary schools:

Exemption is granted from examination in English, or in science, or in geography, history, and civics, to those who complete in an approved institution satisfactory courses, which courses shall have been pursued either during the school year for at least two years, or in a university or normal summer school during at least two six-week sessions, or during one school year and one summer session, and shall have amounted to at least one hundred twenty hours, as follows: In the science of education, sixty hours; and in some branch of literature, science, or art, sixty hours.

NOTES.—(*a*) No exemption is granted for this license from examination in history and principles of education, methods, and school management.

b) The "science of education" will be interpreted to include any professional subjects, namely, principles of education, psychology (educational, applied, genetic, pure), general method, methods of teaching special subjects, school management.

c) No first-year course in foreign languages will be accepted as a satisfactory course in "literature, science, or art;" but second-year and more advanced work will be so accepted.

d) "An approved institution" is interpreted to mean any institution recognized by the Regents as a college or an extension center.

e) No course of less than thirty hours' attendance is accepted.

f) Two thirty-hour courses will not be counted as a sixty-hour course unless they are in closely related subjects; e. g., a thirty-hour course in rhetoric together with a thirty-hour course in advanced French will not count as a sixty-hour course; but a thirty-hour course in rhetoric together with a thirty-hour course in literature will count as a sixty-hour course; so also will a thirty-hour course in methods (general or special) together with a thirty-hour course in school management count as a sixty-hour course.

g) No course is accepted that was not terminated by a successful examination.

h) Exemption is granted only for courses in excess of the studies which were required to establish the eligibility of the applicant for License No. 1.

Principal.—A license as a principal of an elementary school shall qualify the holder for the position of principal of an elementary school, of a truant school, of an elementary evening school, or of an evening high school, provided the licensee holds in the case last mentioned the position of principal of an elementary day school.

NOTES.—A license as principal of an elementary school shall qualify the holder to act as principal of an elementary school having a high-school department, provided he has also at least qualification (*a*) required for license as assistant teacher in a high school.

To be eligible for license as principal in elementary schools, the applicant must have one of the following qualifications:

a) Graduation from a college or university recognized by the Regents of the University of the State of New York, together with at least eight years' successful experience in teaching or supervision. The Master's degree in arts or sciences given as the result of graduate work in a university, may be accepted in lieu of one year of such experience. The Doctor's degree in philosophy or science, given as the result of graduate work in a university, may be accepted in lieu of two years of such experience.

b) Successful experience in teaching or supervision in graded schools for at least ten years, at least five of which must have been in public schools, together with the successful completion of university or college courses satisfactory to the Board of Examiners, such courses to be in pedagogical subjects, and to amount to not less than 120 hours.

1. No exemption for this license is granted from examination in professional subjects or in Group A (English literature, grammar and rhetoric).

2. College graduates are exempted from examination in scholarship, except in Group A.

3. Applicants not graduates of colleges, unless exempted as hereinafter provided, are required to pass, in addition to the examinations mentioned in Sec. 1, an examination in two of the following groups: Group B (logic, psychology), Group C (algebra, geometry, trigonometry), Group D (physics chemistry, physiology, and hygiene), Group E (physical and mathematical geography, United States history, civil government), Group F (a language

and its literature, namely, Greek, Latin, French, German, Spanish, or Anglo-Saxon).

4. Exemption in one or in two of the groups named in Sec. 3 is granted to those who present a diploma or certificate obtained by examination on completion of satisfactory college or university courses.

NOTES.—(*a*) "College or university courses" are interpreted to mean courses pursued under the direction of a college or university and accepted as counting toward a degree.

b) Elementary, i.e., first and second year, courses in modern foreign languages will not be accepted as college courses, nor will preparatory work in ancient languages be so accepted.

c) Each course must extend over at least one year or one summer session.

d) No course of less than thirty hours' attendance is accepted.

e) For exemption in any group, at least sixty hours' attendance must have been given to not more than two of the subjects embraced in such group; two thirty-hour courses will not be counted for exemption in any group, unless the subjects covered by such courses fall within the same group.

f) Exemption is granted only for courses in excess of the studies required to establish the eligibility of applicants for License No. 1.

High-School Teachers.—(1) Junior Teacher: To be eligible for license as junior teacher in high schools, the applicant must have the following qualifications:

Graduation from a college or university recognized by the Regents of the University of the State of New York, together with the completion of a satisfactory pedagogical course of at least one year, or, in lieu of such course, one year's satisfactory experience in teaching in secondary schools.

2) Assistant Teacher: To be eligible for license as assistant teacher in high schools, the applicant must have one of the following qualifications:

a) Graduation from a college or university recognized by the Regents of the University of the State of New York, and not less than three years' satisfactory experience as a teacher or as a laboratory assistant in secondary schools or in colleges. One year of satisfactory post-graduate work resulting in a degree may be accepted in lieu of one year of the required experience in teaching. For applicants for license to teach commercial subjects, or stenography and typewriting, satisfactory experience in business, not exceeding two years in duration, may be accepted in lieu of an equal period in teaching.

b) Graduation from a college or university recognized by the Regents of the University of the State of New York, and two years' satisfactory post-graduate work in the subject in which the applicant seeks a license and in the science of education, and one year of satisfactory experience in teaching in colleges or in secondary schools or in the last two years of elementary schools, which year of experience must not be concurrent with said post-graduate work. For applicants for license to teach commercial subjects, or stenography and typewriting, one year of satisfactory experience in business may be accepted in lieu of the one year of teaching.

c) Graduation from a college or university recognized by the Regents of the University of the State of New York, and five years' satisfactory experience in teaching, at least two of which shall have been in high schools or in the last two years of the New York City public elementary schools. For applicants for license to teach commercial subjects, or stenography and type-writing, satisfactory experience in business, not to exceed three years, may be accepted year for year in lieu of any part of the required experience in teaching.

d) Graduation upon completion of a satisfactory high-school course, or an equivalent academic education; seven years' satisfactory experience in teaching, including either two years of teaching in grades of the last two years of the New York City public elementary schools, or five years of teaching in secondary schools; and the completion of satisfactory university or college courses in the subject in which the applicant seeks a license amounting to not less than 120 hours, at least thirty of which shall have been in the science of education. For applicants for license to teach commercial subjects or stenography and typewriting satisfactory experience in business may be accepted, year for year, in lieu of any part, not exceeding five years, of the required experience in teaching, and satisfactory commercial courses of study may be accepted in lieu of the required college courses.

e) Applicants for license to teach music, art, physical training, or any branch of manual training, may qualify under any of the preceding heads, and also under the following:

Graduation from a satisfactory high-school course, or from an institution of equal or higher rank, and two years of professional training in the subject in which the applicant seeks a license; and four years' satisfactory experience in teaching such special subject. In the case of teachers of manual training, satisfactory experience in shop practice, not to exceed two years, may be accepted in lieu of any equal period of experience in teaching.

3) First Assistant: License as first assistant in high schools may be granted in any of the following subjects: English; classical languages; modern languages; history and civics; economics; biological science; physical science, including physics, chemistry, geography, physiography; mathematics; mechanic arts; fine arts; commercial subjects.

To be eligible for license as first assistant in high schools, the applicant must have one of the following qualifications:

a) Graduation from a college or university recognized by the Regents of the University of the State of New York, and one year's satisfactory post-graduate study, which year may be concurrent with teaching experience; and five years' satisfactory experience in teaching in secondary schools or in colleges, three of which shall have been in the New York City high schools.

b) Graduation from a college or university recognized by the Regents of the University of the State of New York, and one year's satisfactory post-graduate study, which year may be concurrent with teaching experience; and seven years' satisfactory experience in teaching in secondary schools or in colleges. For applicants for license as first assistant in commercial subjects, experience in business satisfactory to the Board of Examiners may be accepted, year for year, in lieu of any part of the required college or post-graduate study.

4) Principal: To be eligible for license as principal in high schools, the applicant must have the following qualifications:

Graduation from a college or university recognized by the Regents of the University of the State of New York, and ten years' satisfactory experience in teaching or supervision, at least five of which must have been in secondary schools, in the position of superintendent or in that of examiner of the city of New York.

Dr. Maxwell reports that a very large proportion of the teaching force is constantly attending lectures in the two universities, and in other approved institutions, with a view to taking degrees and qualifying for the higher licenses in the school system.

Altogether there are fifteen varieties of certificates and each offers an opportunity for the exercise of a different sort of talent in the teacher and while each calls for written examinations in certain subjects, a large part of the credits necessary to obtain an advanced license is given for systematic study carried on through a somewhat lengthy period under teachers of the highest order. If there is any point at which the system seems to be inadequate, it is in that it offers so little encouragement to the teachers who do the work in the important years, one to six inclusive, providing the teachers prefer to remain in the work of these grades. The teachers of these grades form a very large majority of the teaching force.

There are somewhat similar grades of certificates in other school systems, though in none is the plan so fully worked out, and none, so far as reported, has adopted the admirable plan of allowing credits for studies pursued to be substituted for written examinations.

In Baltimore, besides the maximum grade salary which every good teacher may secure, there are other salaries still higher, based on special work or duties partly executive. For example, there are at the present time, twenty positions in preparatory classes carrying a higher salary, twenty-two in special and ungraded classes, nineteen in directing practice work in the training schools, three in grade supervision, one hundred and four in vice-principalships, and twenty-three principalships. There are in all one hundred and ninety-nine of these positions carrying advanced salary in a total of about seventeen hundred elementary-school positions, or about eleven per cent. That is to say, one teacher in every nine is actually occupying a position more remunerative than the regular grade position at the maximum salary for grade work; and, sooner or later, each of the other eight may secure a like reward if, when the opportunity comes, his efficiency is such as to warrant his selection.

The second plan for encouraging teachers to do systematic study is that which reserves certain increases in salary for those who present credentials showing work done along the lines indicated in the rules of the various boards of education. The peculiar advantage of this incentive lies in its direct appeal to every teacher. This plan has been introduced in most cases quite recently and it appears in such a variety of forms that it will be necessary to present several of them in full. In general they are based upon two points, (1) success in schoolroom work and (2) the completion of certain individual lines of study. In several cases, all the details seem to the author to be of such great interest that he has been unwilling to summarize the rules, and has presented them in detail, even at the risk of being somewhat tedious.

A number of cities report plans for recognizing work done in various lines without giving details of the plans. It seems evident that the advance in salaries is adapted to the merits of each case.

Baltimore County allows an increase of $40 per year for work in Baltimore County summer schools or for work in institutions of higher education.

Kansas City (Kan.) holds monthly meetings from 9 to 12 on Saturdays. Each group of teachers takes up a particular topic and carries it through a year. At the end of the year, examinations are held. A record is kept of all the work done by each teacher in any educational line. Promotion in salary depends partly upon this record.

The Lincoln (Neb.) plan is as follows:

"Principals and teachers holding certificates, who have attained the maximum salary within their class, shall receive a special increase of forty-five dollars per year; provided, first, that they shall have taught not less than two years at the maximum salary within their class; second, that they shall have received credit for twenty hours university work in the following subjects: education, literature, history, foreign language, science, English. Of the twenty hours, eight hours shall be required in education; four hours in English. The credit in English is to be based upon the teacher's ability to use correct and effective English and to secure from the pupils results in all phases of English which are satisfactory to the supervision. The remaining hours may be taken in subjects best calculated to meet the needs of the individual teachers.

"Principals and teachers who have attained the first special increase, shall receive the second special increase of forty-five dollars per year; provided, first, that they shall have taught not less than two years at the salary resulting from the first special increase; second, that they shall be rated as highly efficient teachers, by the supervision; third, that they shall receive credit for fifteen hours of university work, or the equivalent, in the following subjects: education, literature, history, foreign languages, science, English. Of the fifteen hours, six hours are required in education and three in English; the credit in English is to be based upon the teacher's ability to use correct and effective English and to secure from her pupils results in all phases of English which are satisfactory to the supervision. The remaining hours may be taken in subjects best calculated to meet the needs of the individual teacher.

"The teachers in high schools are allowed two special increases of forty-five dollars per year each upon similar conditions; the work to be done being especially arranged in each case."

The twenty hours referred to in these rules is about the equivalent of one-sixth of an ordinary four-years college course.

The Cincinnati plan is as follows:

"The Cincinnati University is a civic institution of recognized standing among colleges. It takes students as they pass from high school and gives them a four-year course. In the last two years of the college course, students may elect the training course for teachers in the department which is called the College for Teachers. The Board of Education employs the faculty for this college, spending $10,000 a year upon it. Five instructors are employed. The university professors also give courses especially adapted to the wants of teachers in various lines. Many of these courses are placed at 4 o'clock in the afternoon, and on Saturdays. About 21 of these courses are especially designed for teachers. Last year there were 350 out of 1,000 teachers who took them. This year, each one of the faculty of the College of Teachers, and the professor of geography, are offering a series of 24 conferences with the grade teachers, each taking one grade. These conferences have been very crowded, as many as 110 teachers of a grade applying for the work. In these conferences, selected teachers state what they have done in their grade in nature work or other subjects during the past week, and the matter is then discussed by all. The object is to bring all the teaching of the schools up to the standing of the eight or ten best teachers of the grade, and to prevent stereotyped method by hearing from a variety of good teachers. The conductor works with the teacher who presents the matter so that they are in harmony in their ideas, the conductor really directing the whole trend of thought of the conference.

"From the 1,000 teachers in our schools last year, there were 1,200 professional courses taken by teachers. The year before there were 1,100.

"The incentive to do professional work lies in the provision of the rules of the Board, adopted three years ago, to make the last $50 of the maximum salary dependent upon satisfactory teaching and professional study. Teachers must secure eight credits (not more than two a year) after they have begun teaching, in order to be eligible to the highest salary. In order to remain eligible, they must take professional courses approved by the superintendent, at least every other year; twenty-four meetings a year."

The Boston plan is as follows:

"A plan of promotional examinations has been formulated recently. According to this plan, promotional examinations are held in October and May of each year. These examinations consist of three parts: success in the school during the preceding year; professional study and academic study in some one line. All teachers excepting principals and directors whose salary is on a sliding scale with a fixed increase for each successive year of service, must take the promotional examination next following the anniversary of the date on which they began service. Teachers successfully passing the aforesaid examination shall be placed upon the third year of salary of their respective schedule on the first of January or the first of September next following the date of the examination. Teachers who fail to pass the examination shall remain on the salary of the second year of their respective schedule for another year when they shall again be examined in the same manner. If they successfully pass the examination, they shall be placed upon the third year of salary of their respective schedule, and thereafter shall be advanced regularly on succeeding anniversaries until the sixth year of salary in their respective schedule is reached. Employment of teachers who fail to pass the aforesaid examination on two successive occasions, shall terminate after the first of September next following the date of the second examination.

"Teachers who are receiving the sixth-year salary of their respective schedule shall be examined before being placed upon the seventh year of their respective schedule. This examination consists of three parts: success in school during the preceding year; professional study; academic study in some one line. The teachers who pass this examination shall be regularly advanced on succeeding anniversaries until the maximum salary of their rank or grade is reached. Teachers who fail to pass the aforesaid examination or do not wish to take the examination shall remain on the sixth-year salary of their respective schedules until such time as they have passed this examination.

"Teachers who have successfully passed the two prescribed examinations shall not be required to pass additional promotional examination because of the change of rank.

"Teachers who, on entering the service, are placed on the advanced salary or who are promoted before passing both examinations, shall successfully pass the two prescribed promotional examinations before receiving the maximum salaries of their respective schedules.

"Teachers appointed to begin service prior to September, 1906, are exempt from the preceding regulations relating to promotional examinations excepting that the superintendent shall have authority to require of any teacher in the service to take a promotional examination in May of any year. Teachers failing to pass that examination must again be examined in the following May. The employment of teachers who have been so required to take the promotional examination and who have failed to pass the examination on two successive occasions shall terminate on August 31 next following the date of the second examination."

The following are details of the first of the above mentioned examinations. Those for the second examination have not as yet been formulated:

Success in teaching: Careful attention is given the year preceding examination to the quality of the teachers' work in their classrooms, but no separate or special examination is required to determine their markings in this particular.

Professional subjects, (1) for high-school teachers: first, a written examination, one hour in length, upon methods used by the candidate during the preceding year in teaching any one subject that the candidate shall select; second, a written examination, one hour in length, upon one of a series of pedagogical works concerning phases of secondary education.

2) For all other teachers a similar plan is pursued, namely, a written examination, one hour in length, upon methods of some subject the candidate is engaged in teaching; a written examination, one hour in length, upon some pedagogical work which deals with the line of teaching pursued by the candidate.

For purposes of the examination, the teachers are divided into teachers of grades 5 to 8; teachers of grades 1 to 4; teachers of kindergartens; teachers of special classes; teachers of manual training, sewing, cookery.

Examination in academic subjects, (1) high-school teachers: a written examination one hour in length upon any one of the following subjects not taught by the candidate during the preceding year, that he shall select: history of modern England; Dante's *Divine Comedy;* Goethe's *Faust;* history of music in the 19th century; history of art.   Certain texts are recommended in connection with each subject.

2) For teachers of grades 6 to 8, a written examination, one hour in length, upon any one of the following: American literature; English history as related to American history from 1500 A. D. to 1800 A. D.; physical geography; plane geometry.

3) For teachers of grades 1 to 5, the topics are: history of the United States; geography; mythology—age of fable.

4) For kindergarten teachers, the *Odyssey*.

5) For teachers of special classes, psychology of childhood.

6) For teachers of manual training and sewing, composition and design.

7) For teachers of cookery, chemistry applied to cookery.

In each case, suitable texts are recommended.

The Kansas City (Mo.) plan is as follows:

"With the general movement in 1903 to give our elementary teachers better salaries, the feeling was universal that they should receive for their services adequate compensation.   In the corps there were teachers of all degrees of skill and attainments.   Many had passed the regular examination at the first trial, while no inconsiderable number had carried old passing grades over for three or four examinations in order to secure a permanent certificate. Others, again, who had been appointed subject to examination, had received only temporary permits to teach till the next examination and seemed to stick there.   Under the circumstances, to have granted a uniform flat raise in salaries, thus putting the weak and poorer class of teachers on the same footing as the best teachers on length of service only, would have been in the judgment of the Board and the superintendent, to reduce the entire teaching force to the lowest possible state of inefficiency without any recourse   to recognize skilful and meritorious service.   This would have been the simplest and easiest way out of the difficulty, but the effect, present and prospective, would have been the worst possible on the schools, and it would have permanently crippled, if not paralyzed, the work in every department.   Prior to this agitation the experienced elementary teacher received $65 a month for nine months' work each year.   By action of the Board for all elementary teachers who were receiving $65 a month, or would the next year receive that salary, a flat raise was made to $72 a month. This increased the pay of every $585 teacher to $720 automatically. This was a recognition of term service, but the Board believed in a still further increase of salaries on a scholarship and meritorious service basis. The next step was to work out a system open to all who wished to avail themselves of its provisions, that would enable each teacher by his or her individual effort to receive more salary. After due consideration it was unanimously agreed to by the Board that each teacher whose salary had been advanced to $720 should be entitled to take the first professional examination to be held in September, 1904. Two professional examinations had been decided upon. The first included: history of education, philosophy of education, school management, and English literature. The standard for passing in each of these subjects was seventy per cent. After an applicant had successfully passed the first examination and taught one year, he or she was eligible to the second professional examination, which embraced the same subjects, except that the history of western Europe had been substituted for English literature.

"A committee of four elementary-school principals, two men and two women, was appointed by the Board to conduct the professional examinations. In making out the questions for examinations they were made in groups of ten in each subject, and three distinct questions in each group, so that the applicant had thirty different questions in each group to select from, but limited so as to take one question only from each group. In the four subjects, instead of forty questions, the applicant had one hundred twenty questions to choose from.

"In September, 1904, two hundred ten teachers passed the first professional examination. Those that passed had their salaries raised to $760; that is, two hundred ten teachers received $175 more than they had the year previous. The second examination for this group of teachers was held June, 1905. One hundred seventy-nine passed this examination. After the second professional examination is passed, if the teacher's work is satisfactory, the salary is $825.

"The effect of the professional examinations has been without precedent in any other city of this country, and it is destined to have a very marked influence on the teaching force of many city systems.

"At the outset the examinations met with strenuous opposition. Presently, however, the teachers as a body began to look at the matter from other view-points. Not only would they pass the two professional examinations, but as soon as they got through with the examinations, many of them went to work earnestly to obtain a degree from the State University, and ninety are now engaged in university work through the extension department established in this city by the Board of Curators of the University of Missouri. When they began to prepare for the professional examinations so many new activities were set in motion in their minds and so many new lines of thought and broader vistas of historical and philosophical knowledge opened up to them, that they organized themselves into a compact working body, and then they began regular courses of study to perfect themselves in scholarship, knowledge, and power. This is, indeed, the very highest tribute to their energy, sane thinking, and substantial views of real progress.

"Intentionally, the maximum salary for elementary teachers was not closed at the bottom, but left open at the top. Those who go automatically to $720 are under no compulsion to get out of that class unless they desire to do so. But few ambitious teachers, however, are willing to stop there."

Although no city reported more elaborate or a greater variety of agencies of the usual sort for the improvement of teachers, such as institutes, voluntary organizations, teachers', meetings, principals' meetings, than did Kansas City, so that the ordinary incentives toward improvement have here received a most thorough test, yet the report from that city contains the following:

"The influence that more than any other one thing has stimulated study among the teachers, is the professional examination. It came upon them much in the nature of an earthquake or a tidal wave, with the result that a new system has replaced the old. It put the city schools twenty years ahead of themselves at one step. It has produced a different attitude of mind among the majority of our teachers."

The Baltimore plan is as follows:

In rearranging the salary schedule the Board has finally been able to provide a respectable minimum salary of $504 per annum, which all teachers of promise reach after one successful year as regularly elected teachers. The way is then open to each for an advance to $700 per annum in increments given annually for five years upon satisfactory evidence of efficiency and progress. The special kind of progress required for advance from $504 to $600 is increased skill in English. This is tested by an examination. For a year or two after leaving the City Training School no line of professional study for the young teacher will, we think, yield results as useful to the school system as study tending toward accuracy and facility in the use of the mother tongue. The examination in English for 1907 is explained in the following:[2]

PROMOTIONAL EXAMINATION, PART I—ENGLISH

The rule for the first advance of teachers' salaries beyond $504 (Promotional Examination, Part I) prescribes as one requirement "an impersonal test in the correct and effective use and interpretation of English." It is a well-known fact that many students secure a satisfactory general average of scholarship at graduation from the high school when their equipment and power in English are not at that time equal to a teacher's needs; yet such graduates frequently develop afterwards into very good teachers. All candidates for the first promotion in the teaching service should be able to show that since their graduation from the high school they have attained that sound judgment and refined taste in English which is the outcome of wider reading and study and greater maturity of mind than can be expected in high-school students. The examination in English, therefore, is set for the purpose of ascertaining (1) whether the teacher's own hold upon English is satisfactory; and (2) whether the teacher is in possession of some good aims and methods for the instruction of children in English composition and literature.

A teacher should be able to speak and write English with absolute correctness, and also to interpret correctly any ordinary piece of classic poetry or prose. This requirement, though, is not extensive enough; for in fact quite meager attainments suffice to make one simply correct in the use and understanding of English. Many persons speak and write in a way that is not incorrect; but their

[2] Taken from Supt. J. H. Van Sickle's report.

English is decidedly ineffective. Mere correctness in English is not enough to insure success in teaching.

To succeed in the classroom one's words must be effective; and effective English, does not come unsought. For the production of effective English the teacher needs all the art that can be mustered. Similarly, the teacher must be able not only to understand classic literature, but also to interpret it effectively to children; and expertness in interpretation can be secured only by systematic study.

As it is necessary for the teacher to have an effective command of English, and as it is improbable that he can gain such command without deliberate study and practice, it would seem that any candidate for promotion ought to be more than willing to show that he has pursued a course in English comprehensive enough to include a review of grammar; a good introduction into rhetoric, accompanied by sufficient practice in composition; and a careful study of a number of English classics.

Particular texts are named in order to offer to teachers who desire to make definite preparation for this examination a specific set of books to work upon. It must, however, always be remembered that no talismanic character resides in any selection of texts; others would serve quite as well.

The aim of any course in English is not primarily informational, to make one acquainted with particular pieces of literature; it is disciplinary and cultural, to create in one by the intensive study of a certain number of classics some critical insight and some literary power. Consequently the texts here selected are taken intentionally from those authors that are known to every well-read person, so that the candidate will not be burdened with the task of studying up a mass of new subject-matter; but will on the contrary need simply to make ready for some interpretative work upon classics with which he is already familiar. It is to be noted further that in no case will the memorizing of minute details be deemed sufficient to outweigh poor judgment or illogical reasoning.

The special kind of progress which we wish next to emphasize is the ability to discover problems in the work one is actually doing so that the professional growth may occur through the doing of each day's work in a professional way. Satisfactory evidence of such progress may be submitted at any time after the advance to $600 has been realized. It consists of an essay and discussion, a classroom demonstration, and an examination on two professional books.

PROMOTIONAL EXAMINATION, PART II—STUDY OF A SPECIAL PROBLEM

It will be observed that the promotional requirement for teachers of experience is not an examination in the ordinary sense of that term. It is given not at all for the purpose of finding out how much teachers know, and not wholly to find out what they can do. It has a dynamic purpose: to direct attention to problems which press for solution, and to cultivate in teachers a tendency to deal with these problems in a thoughtful way.

All teachers after receiving a salary of $600 for one year, provided they are competent to teach the regular subjects of their respective grades, may become eligible to receive a salary of $700 per annum by passing the second part of the promotional examination, which is defined as follows:

The Promotional Examination, Part II, shall consist of (*a*) a written report of the working out of some problem of teaching or the study of a particular group of children; (*b*) such a defense of the report before a board of examiners, consisting of the superintendent and two other members selected by him, as will evince familiarity with educational literature bearing on the problem or study; and, when required, (*c*) a classroom demonstration before a board similarly composed.

It will be observed that the rule defines the essay as "a written report of the working out of some problem of teaching, or the study of a particular group of children." This means that the teacher is not expected to prepare an abstract or academic discussion having no relation to his own classroom problems. The essay should, on the contrary, grow out of the candidate's actual teaching; so that, instead of his being distracted from practical problems while working for the promotional examination, he shall be the more intently studying his daily work. And in case the examiners think that an essay has been written with too little reference to the candidate's actual teaching, they will feel at liberty to call for the "classroom demonstration," in which it must be shown that the candidate was not merely theorizing in his essay.

Teachers need not hesitate to attempt such essays as are contemplated in the rule. No great display of learning is expected, but only a clear and simple presentation of everyday schoolroom experiences that have had some educational significance for the writer. To the observant teacher, who is really trying to understand the forty children committed to his care, every school day affords such experiences; and his experiences will not exactly duplicate those of any other teacher, for his children are in many particulars unlike any other children. His observations may tend to verify or contradict what he has previously read or thought; and in either case he will be led to read further in books that treat of the aspect of teaching which has attracted his interest. Out of such reading and observation and thought will come ideas well worth being committed to writing; and these when clearly and definitely stated will doubtless form an acceptable essay. Or a teacher may secure permission to apply to his class some special plan of teaching or governing, and from his day-to-day records of this plan draw up an interesting and instructive discussion. Or why should not a teacher undertake to throw light upon classroom problems by showing how one or another procedure appears from the child's point of view? Let him show, for example, how the child is affected by this or that attitude on the teacher's part, or by this or that requirement in discipline or study. This would certainly involve "the study of a particular group of children," and would therefore, if well done, fully satisfy the requirement. Hundreds of teachers have experiences just as interesting and just as worthy of permanent record as many of those which have in recent years found a ready market in the form of magazine articles. In fact, there are as many ways of satisfying the essay requirement as there are different tastes and aptitudes among teachers; and every good teacher is sure to become a better teacher by undertaking from time to time some such composition.

The essay when presented must be accompanied by an outline showing the trend of the argument and the conclusions reached, and by a list of the books consulted in making the study. From the list of books the candidate will submit for approval two, upon which will be based the discussion that "will evince familiarity with educational literature bearing on the problem or study." As a special caution on the use of authorities in preparing the essay, it is recommended that candidates indulge but little, if at all, in quotations. Quotations often produce the effect of needless and obstructive insertions in an otherwise straightforward and coherent discussion: and they also tend frequently to make an argument appear less sincere than if the writer had set it forth in his own style. But in case a candidate considers it necessary, at a particular point, to insert a quotation, he should at least attach a foot-note citing his authority by title and page. It may be added that such slight modification of another writer's sentence as the alteration of a word or two, does not relieve one of the obligation of acknowledging the source.

As a teacher's classroom work must be entirely satisfactory when he comes up in Promotional Examination, Part II, he may get a preliminary judgment on his teaching before he undertakes his essay or at any time during its composition. Under the rules governing advance in salaries, the concurrence of the superintendent with the principal in a favorable judgment, is required.

The formal report upon the actual class work of a candidate in this examination cannot be made until the other conditions set by the rule have been met; but the candidate is of course entitled to timely information as to whether his teaching is likely to be approved under the requirements for advance to the maximum salary.

The following are a few topics of papers in Promotional Examination Part II. They are taken at random: Self Governing History Classes (by a teacher in a departmental group) ; The Teaching of Reading to non-English-Speaking Children; Seat Work in its Relation to the Recitation; Departmental Teaching in a Three-Teacher Group; A German Primer (MS of a book actually prepared for publication by a teacher of first grade in an English-German School; it was fully illustrated and accompanied by a chart—much superior to book in use) ; Everyday Difficulties in Teaching Beginners Latin; Use and Abuse of the Study Period; Foreign Travel as an Aid in Teaching Geography; The Ungraded Class; The Service of Music in the Schoolroom; Two Months of Experiment in Combining Individual, Sectional, and Class Methods of Teaching; The Argument from Experience in Introducing High-School Subjects into the Upper Grammar Grades; Group Teaching; Flexible Grading; Use of Games in Teaching French and German to Children in Seventh and Eighth Grades (the teacher invented several games).

It is difficult to imagine work that would be of more value professionally to a teacher than that of preparing during her actual teaching of a given subject such a study of that subject as these topics suggest.

When the present salary schedule was adopted, teachers of five years' experience in the Baltimore schools who had been rated as good teachers by their respective principals for the three successive years immediately preceding were declared exempt from the English examination and were at once advanced to $600 per annum. Those not so rated by their principals, ninety-seven in number, were required to make such improvement in their work as would justify a satisfactory rating before they could receive the increase; but they were informed that they, like the others, would receive it without examination whenever they secured the required record, and that all necessary assistance would be given them. Grade supervision became absolutely necessary at this point. In no other way, except by actual attendance at a training school, could any of these teachers have received sufficient assistance. To be effective in such cases the help must be expert and individual. It must fit the case. Accordingly, expert teachers selected as grade supervisors were assigned by the superintendent to represent him in learning the special needs of this class of teachers and in helping them in every possible way. The supervisors were left entirely unhampered by any special instructions from the superintendent. Each bore a letter of introduction, but as a matter of fact, the letter was seldom presented to the teacher, a few informal words bringing about freer relations. Nevertheless it has proved invaluable in cases where the personality of the teacher visited seemed to indicate that a formal business footing would be more agreeable to her.

The supervisors sought to indicate selection of subject-matter, methods of presenting it, and methods of discipline. They worked out entire plans for the use of the teachers, following this by helping them to work out other plans and, a later step, by sending suggestions for improvement of plans which these teachers sent to them by mail. This individual work was supplemented, whenever possible by a general teachers' meeting.

The result of this plan of working individually with teachers who had failed to make good under general supervision is that sixty-eight out of the ninety-seven have been pronounced good by the same principals who had not previously felt justified in making a favorable report.

Too much cannot be said in commendation of the way in which these teachers as a body co-operated with the supervisors in working out special problems in their individual rooms—the frank statement of their own difficulties, the good will with which they joined the supervisors in meeting these difficulties, and the hard work they put on any indicated plan. It must be distinctly understood that, while they very naturally and properly wished for the increase in salary which improved work would bring, they were not limited by this view, but endeavored to attain a higher grade of work for its own sake.

Similar work is needed annually with a large number of the newer teachers who are endeavoring to secure a record in classroom work that will make them eligible to take Promotional Examination, Part I, and with an equally large number who are anxious about the "classroom demonstration," which is a factor in Part II. These teachers wish to get assurance in advance of the examination that if they enter it, their record in classroom work will not hold them back. The grade supervision attempted thus far has been of this special nature; it has had some definite purpose to accomplish. Put upon this basis, grade supervision is a welcome help. The supervisor comes as a friend who has no other purpose than an endeavor to aid the teacher in reaching a desired goal.

The Chicago (Ill.) plan is as follows:

Teachers may be promoted to higher groups of salaries in any one of three ways: (1) by submitting evidence of the completion of the required study courses, either in the Normal Extension Department or in some degree-conferring institution, pp. 55–62; (2) by taking examinations in the study courses referred to above; (3) by taking the promotional examination. This examination, in the case of elementary teachers, consists of two papers, one in professional study, and one in some academic subject. In the case of principals, teachers in high schools, and teachers in normal practice schools, the examination consists of one paper in professional study.

Of these plans for the advancement of teachers, the one based upon examinations is the oldest. When it was adopted it immediately caused a great demand for instructors in the various subjects in which examinations could be taken. In order to meet this demand, the Board of Education undertook a line of work which has been productive of most remarkable results, viz., that of normal extension. The plan in brief is this: The Board of Education agrees to furnish to any group of teachers of fifteen or more, in any part of the city, an instructor in any of the lines of work for which credit is given. Many of these classes meet in various halls in the central part of the city, the expenses of the rental of these halls being paid by the Board of Education. Other classes meet at the Normal School and in schoolrooms scattered throughout the city. These classes may meet at 4 o'clock in the afternoon of any school day excepting Monday, and at any hour between 9 and 12 on Saturday morning.

The first classes organized were largely institute classes of one hour each conducted chiefly on the lecture plan. It was found that the method and the length of the recitation period were not productive of the highest degree of efficiency from the standpoint of real scholarship. With the adoption of the plan for credits for work done in the normal-extension classes, the institute classes have been practically abandoned, the teachers themselves finding that they could get the work they needed more satisfactorily in the twenty-four recitations of one and one-half hours each than in the thirty-six lectures of one hour each.

The study class has certain advantages which are lacking from other forms of work undertaken for teachers, such as lectures, institutes, and grade meetings, in that the study class calls for vigorous application, serious, long-continued intellectual effort on the part of the teacher. In the lecture system of instruction, whether the lecture is a single one delivered by some great leader of thought or whether the lectures are arranged in a series as in the ordinary institute, the hearers are in a receptive attitude, while in the study class, those who undertake the work give forth to their teachers, the results of their mental activity. From the lecture, the ordinary listener carries away at best only a few suggestions and a certain amount of spiritual uplift. What one has gained by hard study and has reproduced in oral or written form for criticism has not only become a permanent possession to the student but has also increased his mental power.

Rules of the Chicago Board of Education Relating to Promotional Examinations

CLASSIFICATION OF SALARIES IN ELEMENTARY SCHOOLS

There shall be a schedule of salaries for teachers in the elementary schools, which shall include two groups of salaries:

The first group of the schedule shall provide for additional advance in salary year by year for teachers who have reached the maximum salary of the second group, and who shall have complied with the conditions named below.

ADVANCEMENT FROM SECOND TO FIRST GROUP

The conditions governing advancement from the second to the first group of salaries for elementary teachers and head assistants shall be as follows:

Elementary teachers.—Teachers shall be promoted from the second to the first group by a vote of the Board of Education, upon a recommendation of the superintendent of schools. Those teachers shall be eligible for such recommendation and promotion who have served a year at the maximum salary of the second group, and whose average in efficiency as shown by the records in the superintendent's office shall be eighty per cent. or above, and who shall attain an average of eighty per cent. or above in the following tests:

a) An examination to test the work and interest of the teacher in the lines of professional study and training, including the subjects of school management, pedagogy, psychology, and the history of education.

b) An examination to test the work and interest of the teacher in any one of the following fields of academic work:

English language and literature; general history; physical science; biological science; foreign languages (Latin, Greek, German, French, Spanish); algebra and geometry; music; drawing;

manual training; household arts; geography (covering physical, mathematical, and commercial geography, with geology) ; physical culture (covering anatomy and physiology, theory of gymnastics, method of teaching, preparation of sets of exercises for different grades, and practical work).

The credit given to the professional examinations shall be twice that given to the academic examinations, and an average mark of eighty per cent. shall be required of all teachers passing these tests. The final mark shall be made up of three items, which shall receive equal credit, as follows:

a) Efficiency mark for the preceding year, as equalized by the Board of District Superintendents,

b) Mark obtained on the professional study paper of the promotional examination, and

c) Mark obtained on the academic paper of the promotional examination, provided that no examination mark below seventy shall be considered, and provided further that, if a candidate divides the examination, the paper taken in the preliminary part shall not be credited in the final average unless the candidate has a mark of eighty or over on such paper.

Elementary teachers who have arrived at the maximum salary of the second group, who meet the other requirements of the schedule, and who possess an elementary principal's certificate, shall be admitted to the first group without examination. Elementary teachers who have arrived at the maximum salary of the second group, who meet the other requirements of the schedule, and possess a certificate to teach in the high schools, shall be advanced to the first group upon passing the professional examination only. Elementary teachers who have arrived at the maximum salary of the second group, who meet the other requirements of the schedule, and who possess certificates to teach music, drawing, German, household arts, or manual training, shall be advanced to the first group upon passing the professional examination only.

Teachers of physical culture, teachers of manual training, and teachers of household arts in elementary schools, teachers in kindergartens and teachers of the deaf, whose mark of efficiency is eighty or above, and who have reached the maximum salary in the second group, shall be eligible, for admission to the promotional examination provided for the regular teachers in elementary schools, and upon passing it shall be promoted to Group I, it being understood that the academic subject chosen for the promotional examination by the holder of a special certificate shall not be the same subject as that in which the special certificate was granted.

The schedules of salaries for high-school teachers and for principals of elementary schools are arranged in three groups.

High-school teachers.—High-school teachers who have reached the maximum salary of the third group, whose average in efficiency as shown by the records in the superintendent's office shall be eighty per cent. or above shall be advanced to the second group after passing an examination in methods of teaching the subjects in which they give instruction. High-school teachers who have served a year at the maximum salary of the second group, whose average in efficiency as shown by the records in the superintendent's office shall be eighty per cent. or above, shall be advanced to the first group upon passing an examination in school management, psychology, pedagogy, and the history of education. No high-school teacher shall be eligible to the principalship of a high school who has not taken the professional examination required of candidates for the first group.

Principals.—Principals of elementary schools who have served a year at the maximum salary in the third group, whose average in efficiency as shown by the records in the superintendent's office shall be eighty per cent. or above, shall be permitted to advance to the second group of salaries upon passing an examination in school management, and methods of instruction in primary and grammar grades. Principals who have served a year at the maximum salary in the second group, whose average in efficiency as shown by the records in the superintendent's office shall be eighty per cent. or above, shall be permitted to advance to the first group of salaries upon passing an examination in professional work, including school management, psychology, pedagogy, and the history of education; provided, that nothing in this schedule shall be construed as abolishing the restriction upon the salaries of principals on account of the membership of the schools, as provided elsewhere.

Teachers in normal practice schools.—The conditions governing the advancement of teachers in the practice schools from the second to the first group of salaries shall be as follows:

Teachers shall be promoted from the second to the first group by a vote of the Board of Education, upon a recommendation of the superintendent of schools. Teachers shall be eligible for such recommendation and promotion who shall have received the maximum salary of the second group for one year, and whose efficiency mark as a critic teacher shall be eighty-five per cent., or above, for the year preceding the promotional examination to which they shall be eligible for admission, and who shall obtain an average of eighty per cent., or above, in a promotional examination, which shall be based upon the work of expert critic teaching. Teachers who are transferred from any of the grades in the elementary schools to the practice schools, who have previously taken a promotional examination and are in the first group of salaries there, shall be placed in the first group of salaries for teachers in the practice schools.

Promotion of special teachers in the normal practice schools.— Salaries of special teachers of manual training, physical culture, and household arts in the normal practice schools shall be the same as the like positions in the other elementary schools and the schedule of salaries shall apply in these practice schools as in all parts of the city, except that such special teachers assigned to these practice schools shall be classed as critic teachers, and the promotion by examination from the second group to the first shall be according to the rules applying to critic teachers.

Study-Course Plan for Promotion

Teachers, head assistants, and principals who are eligible for promotion shall be allowed, if they so elect, to substitute five courses of study of not less than twenty-four lessons of one and one-half hours each, or thirty-six lessons of one hour each, for the examination requirements contained in the "Rules and Regulations of the Board of Education." Such courses of study offered for advancement to a higher group shall be pursued under the direction of the Chicago Normal School, or in some accredited institution of learning authorized by law to confer academic degrees. Courses of study pursued in such degree-giving institutions may be accepted for credit toward advancement to a higher group, upon approval of such institutions by the principal of the Chicago Normal School and the superintendent of schools, but no courses of study shall be so accepted which are not superior in grade to the work of the Chicago public high schools. Such courses of study shall be deemed successfully completed when the proper official of the institution shall certify in writing that said course has been satisfactorily completed, and when such report has been approved by the principal of the Normal School and the superintendent of schools; provided, that if such course has been taken in a degree-giving institution, such official shall also certify that said course has been credited in said institution toward the attainment of an academic degree. The superintendent of schools and the principal of the Chicago Normal School shall have authority to take such steps as they deem necessary to satisfy themselves of the satisfactory nature and completion of these courses.

In determining the eligibility of elementary teachers for advancement to a higher group, credit shall be allowed upon the following basis, a general average of eighty per cent. being required:

Efficiency marks for the preceding school year, as given by the principal and one district superintendent, and equalized by the Board of District Superintendents, 5 credits; five courses of study successfully completed, one credit each, 5 credits; total, 10 credits.

Any teacher desiring to do so may substitute a written examination based on the work outlined in any one of the groups of subjects of study authorized under this rule for one or more of the five courses of study required, provided that the mark obtained in each of such examinations shall not be less than seventy-five per cent. in which case the teacher shall receive for said examination the credit belonging to the course of study for which it is substituted. Elementary teachers who comply with the other requirements of this rule, and who possess certificates to teach music, drawing, German, household arts, or manual training, shall be credited with two and one-half courses toward advancement to a higher group of salaries.

Teachers of physical culture, household arts, and manual training in the elementary schools, teachers in kindergartens, and teachers of the deaf shall be eligible for advancement to a higher group, upon conditions similar to those required of teachers in elementary schools, provided that any courses of study or examinations offered in subjects in which their special certificates were granted shall be of an advanced nature.

Teachers in high schools and principals of elementary schools shall be eligible for advancement from the third to the second group, upon conditions similar to those required of teachers in elementary schools, provided that no course of study or examination shall be accredited to any teacher in a high school or principal of an elementary school, unless said work is such as would be accepted for the degree of Master of Arts by an accredited institution authorized to confer said degree. Teachers in high schools and principals of elementary schools shall be eligible for advancement from the second to the first group upon conditions similar to those required for advancement from the third to the second group, provided that the courses of study or examinations offered for advancement to the first group, including any previously offered for advancement from the third to the second group, shall be equal in amount to a year's work such as would be accepted for the degree of Master of Arts by an accredited institution authorized to confer said degree. And provided further, that after June 30, 1907, no teacher in a high school or principal of an elementary school shall be eligible for advancement to the first group unless his efficiency average for the preceding school year is eighty-five or over for the year preceding that in which the examination was taken. In addition to the principal's efficiency mark each high-school teacher shall be given a mark by another supervisory officer.

The courses of study provided for in the above rule shall be elected from courses included in the following groups of subjects:

Education, including history and philosophy of education, school organization, science and art of instruction, special method, and educational ideals and classics.

Psychology, including introductory psychology, genetic and functional psychology, psychology applied to education, comparative psychology, the psychology of special subjects, and the psychology of abnormal, sub-normal, and defective children.

Mathematics, solid geometry, college algebra, trigonometry, analytics, and calculus.

Physical Science, including physics and chemistry.

Geographical Science, including physical, mathematical, political, and commercial geography, geology, and geographic drawing.

Biological Science, including zoölogy, botany, physiology, hygiene, and nature-study.

Physical Education, including applied anatomy, the physiology of exercise, and gymnastic history, theory, and practice.

Music, including both vocal and instrumental music, elementary harmony and composition, and the history of music.

English Language and Literature, including grammar, composition, rhetoric, oral reading, the study of English and American authors, and of literary types, periods, movements, and history.

Foreign Language, Latin, Greek, French, German, or Spanish, including literature, grammar, composition, and the history of the language and literature.

History, including the history of the United States, the mediaeval and modern history of European countries, and the history of the ancient world.

Political Science, including civics, economics, sociology, and industrial history.

Art, including drawing, composition and design, color, the study of masterpieces of historic and modern art, the history and philosophy of art, constructive design, and mechanical drawing.

Manual Training, including work in wood, paper, cardboard, leather, metal, textiles, weaving, basketry, clay-modeling, bookbinding, applied design, constructive and mechanical design, and the history and philosophy of manual training and the science of its materials.

Sewing, including drafting and pattern-making; cutting, sewing, fitting, constructing, and repairing simple garments; also the study of textiles and fabrics; and the principles of design, proportion, and color harmony.

Cookery and Dietetics, including the structure, composition, preparation, and serving of foods; food materials and their values and uses; dietetics; and hygienic cookery.

No course of study or examination taken in the normal extension department prior to September, 1904, or in degree-giving institutions prior to passing the last examination for promotion in Chicago, or prior to the assignment in the Chicago public schools of the teacher or principal offering it, shall be accredited under this rule, excepting that any teacher who has not yet completed the promotional examination, but who has credit for one subject in that examination, shall be credited with two and one-half courses toward advancement to a higher group. A teacher or principal who has received credit under these rules for a course of study or examination shall not receive an additional credit for the completion of the same course of study or examination a second time. No teacher shall be permitted to enroll in more than two courses in any one school year, but this restriction shall not apply to courses taken in the summer term of the Normal School. At least one of the said courses or examinations offered by any teacher or principal for advancement to a higher group shall have been taken and satisfactorily completed within the two years next preceding the promotion of said teacher.

The fact that a high-school teacher is in the second group will be considered evidence that he or she has completed the requirements for promotion from Group III to Group II, namely, five courses of study of not less than thirty-six hours each.

For promotion from Group II to Group I the rule requires (including the five courses offered for promotion from Group III to Group II) one year's work of a grade which will be accepted in any approved degree-giving institution toward the degree of Master of Arts. One year's work in such institutions is usually understood to be nine courses of study aggregating about 430 hours.

Any course which is accepted by an approved degree-giving institution toward the attainment of the degree of Master of Arts will be accepted toward this promotion, whether it is technically listed in the graduate schools or in the senior colleges.

College courses aggregating a number of hours equal to the number of hours required in four courses of study of thirty-six hours each will be accepted as the equivalents of such courses.

The work offered should not, however, cover more than two general subjects.

The same ruling is held applicable to elementary principals.

One of the fundamental ideas of this promotional plan is that it tends to keep teachers in touch with modern scholarship. Because of this, attention is called to the provision to the effect that "At least one of the said courses or examinations offered by any teacher or principal for advancement to a higher group shall have been taken and satisfactorily completed within the two years next preceding the promotion of said teacher."

All regularly assigned teachers in the public, parochial, or private schools of Chicago are eligible to attend these classes. Substitutes and cadets are not eligible to enroll. Other teachers not connected regularly with any school are not eligible to attend.

Analysis of Conditions for Promotion

A. TEACHERS IN ELEMENTARY SCHOOLS, AND HEAD ASSISTANTS

I. *Eligibility.*—A teacher must have an efficiency mark of eighty or over for the preceding school year, separate marks to be given by the principal and a District Superintendent, and the two to be revised by the Board of District Superintendents.

II. *Promotion.*—A teacher may take either (1) an examination, her final mark to be determined as follows: (a) efficiency mark as above, one-third, (b) mark on professional study paper, one-third, (c) mark on academic paper, one-third; or (2) five study courses of twenty-four lessons (one and one-half hours each) or thirty-six lessons (one hour each), to be pursued under the direction of the normal extension department, or in some institution authorized by law to confer academic degrees; five credits to be given for the teacher's efficiency mark, as above, and five credits for the successful completion of the five courses of study; no teacher to take more than two classes a year, and at least one course to be taken within the two years preceding promotion.

III. *Study Classes.*—Teachers may take their work either (1) in Normal Extension classes in the afternoons or on Saturday mornings from October to April; or (2) in the four weeks' summer term of the Chicago Normal School, classes to be given six days a week, in two daily periods of one and one-half hours each; or (3) in any institution authorized by law to confer academic degrees.

B. PRINCIPALS OF ELEMENTARY SCHOOLS AND TEACHERS IN HIGH SCHOOLS

I. *Eligibility.*—For promotion to the second group a principal or high-school teacher must have an efficiency mark of eighty or over for the preceding school year, and for promotion to the first group a mark of eighty-five or over.

II. *Promotion.*—A principal or high-school teacher may take either (1) an examination on professional subjects; or (2) five study courses in advanced work at any institution authorized by law to confer academic degrees.

The extent of the work which has grown out of this plan is partly shown in the following:

REPORT OF NORMAL EXTENSION CLASSES FOR WEEK ENDING DEC. 14, 1907

Subjects Study Classes	No. Classes	Attendance	Membership	Average attendance per class
Education	4	192	226	48
Psychology	6	177	196	30
Mathematics	2	39	46	20
Science	8	235	292	29
Geography	6	132	170	22
History	5	88	99	18
English	12	279	326	23
German	5	156	170	31
French	9	212	270	24
Spanish	3	34	53	11
Art	31	844	1045	27
Music	11	379	458	34
Physical education	4	224	254	56
Manual training	12	311	357	27
Cookery	3	87	87	29
Sewing	15	308	492	20
Industrial art	40	1289	1521	32
Kindergarten	2	57	72	29
Total	177	5043	6134	28

The following table shows the number of persons enrolled in extension classes at the close of the year 1906–7:

Elementary teachers 3,228
High-school teachers 46
Principals of elementary schools........................ 28
Special teachers 29
                                                        ————
    Total public-school teachers 3,331
Parochial-school teachers 21
Private-school teachers 21
Unassigned 11
                                                  ——— 53
                                                        ————
Total enrolled 3,384

Of the above the following number of persons are enrolled in
two classes:

Elementary teachers 857
High-school teachers 9
Principals of elementary schools........................ 8
Special teachers 5
                                                        ————
    Total public-school teachers........................ 879
Parochial-school teachers 4
Private-school teachers 4
                                                  ——— 8
                                                        ————
Total number of students in two classes................. 887
Total number enrolled in Extension classes during fall
    term of 1907–8 7,456

The total expenditure for this work for the year ending De-
cember 31, 1907, was $16,032.18. This does not include cost of
heat, light and janitor service in school buildings.

It will be noted from the above schedule that in the selection of
studies those are most frequently chosen which have an immediate
effect upon the school work. This has a good and a bad side. It
shows the eagerness of the teacher to turn her work to account in
improving the character of her teaching. It would be better in
some ways, if her studies were partly those which took her out
of her immediate lines of work, those which induced her to enter
more scholarly fields of study.

In addition to the above classes many courses are being pursued by teachers in the various colleges and art schools in or near the city.

Certain other interesting phases of work are mentioned in the reports, some of which are the following:

State Inspector George B. Aiton of the Minnesota high schools recommends that the colleges and normal schools of a given state or a given section of the country arrange uniform study courses for the various grades of teachers in the country and the smaller cities and offer these courses through correspondence with the plan that these courses when satisfactorily completed shall be credited towards diplomas of graduation from normal schools or universities, or toward higher degrees.

A most important work is that undertaken by the Chicago Normal School in the publication of a bi-monthly magazine devoted to the consideration of various phases of modern educational thought. The magazine is edited by Mrs. Ella Flagg Young, principal of the Normal School. The articles are written by members of the Normal School faculty and educators of high standing from other institutions throughout the country. These articles form the basis for part of the study in the Normal School. The magazine is supplied to all of the city schools and in many of them furnishes material for the meetings of the principal with the teachers.

Teachers in the Horace Mann School, New York, and in a few of the other schools reporting may take professional courses in the near-by colleges without expense. It might be well for boards of education generally to agree to pay the tuition of teachers doing work in neighboring institutions of learning.

Several cities report the establishment of an eligible list for appointment. In Boston the appointments are made from the highest three on the list. In Chicago from the list taken in order of rank. In Chicago, in the case of experienced teachers, rank on the eligible list is determined by the average of the mark obtained in examinations with the mark obtained in sub-stitute service. In the case of graduates of the Chicago Normal School, rank is determined by taking the average of the mark given for the two years' course in the Normal School and the mark obtained in cadet or substitute service during the four months' probation.

In Boston, a teacher may, at the end of the seventh year of service, be given a leave of absence on half-pay for, one year of study or travel. In Chicago, a teacher may obtain at any time, a year's leave (but without salary) for study, or leave for travel up to four months.

In a number of cities, the principals are required to record at certain intervals their estimate of the teachers under their charge. This has indirect influence on the work of the teachers and of the principals. It is necessary that the principal should continually study his teachers in order to help them, and the fact that he must record his estimate helps him in making his judgment. The principal is required to estimate the work of the teacher, in such points as ability to discipline, ability to teach, to co-operate with the principal and other teachers, scholarly habits, devotion to duty, etc.

Several cities report much good obtained from magazine clubs which make a study of the current educational literature.

Newark (N. J.) reports:

"Our Public Library is in close touch with every school in the city and supplies any needed material, prepares and classifies lists of books needed from time to time to carry out and elucidate the course of study. It also holds frequent school exhibits for the benefit of the teachers. It publishes from time to time valuable information, monographs, etc., for distribution among teachers."

TO SUMMARIZE

The work of making good teachers must be carried forward steadily because of the immaturity of teachers on entering the profession, the unevenness of their preparation, the singular lack of external stimulus connected with the practice of the profession, the complex nature of the work that must be intrusted to even the poorest teacher, the profound injury that results when the work is badly done, the constant change in methods and curriculum.

The making of good teachers is accomplished in two ways, by instruction on the part of the supervision, by personal study on the part of the teacher. Instruction and study may be concerned with information, with methods or with principles. The instruction which comes through sympathetic supervision which suggests correct methods but does not impose particular ones, which points to principles underlying methods, which shows the application of principles to schoolroom practice, which arouses a love for excellence in work and in scholarship will ever be the most powerful of the agencies for good.

The instruction which comes from lectures, whether by great men or small, whether in ambitious lecture courses, in university extension courses or in ordinary institutes is of doubtful value. The hearer plays simply a passive, receptive, part; he listens to a brief summary of a more or less profound study of a given subject and knowing nothing of the background of the subject, this summary makes but little permanent impression. He goes away with a pleasing sensation of having learned something and the knowledge lasts but little longer than the sensation.

This training of teachers after they enter the work is deserving of much greater consideration than it has heretofore received. Many of the reports show an attitude of hopelessness regarding the mediocre teacher. To tolerate this attitude is to acknowledge defeat. It results in a cessation of effort to help on the part of the supervision and a placid self-satisfaction that tends toward mental death on the part of the teacher.

The school should be made the unit. The principal should be made responsible for the teaching of all subjects. The departmental plan makes this possible and provides for the teacher an incentive and an opportunity for scholarly preparation. There are undeveloped talents in every corps of teachers.

The principal must be acquainted with the work of the normal school and point out to young teachers the application of the principles of teaching, otherwise much of the work of the normal school will be lost. Normal extension classes have a similar office.

After wise supervision, the great essential for a teacher's life and growth is vigorous, systematic study. It is the duty of principal and superintendent to stimulate this study in every possible way. By example, by suggestion, by promotion, by increase of salary.

Promotion and increase of salary are the rights of the conscientious scholarly teacher and the expectation of these advantages the greatest spur to the indolent. In the demonstration of this proposition lies the chief value of the present study. The various plans for attaining this result presented herein deserve the most careful consideration.

In small communities where the homes of teachers are near together, much may be done in study classes led by the superintendent or his assistants. As the city grows,, the teachers in a given school or a given neighborhood may reside far apart from one another and the difficulty of gathering them together for systematic work increases. It thus becomes more and more important that contact with the supervision should come largely in school hours and that a teacher at other times should be left free to study when and where she can do so most conveniently The amount of this study at any time need not, ought not be great, but it should be constant, thorough and ever advancing into widening fields.

REPORT OF THE SECRETARY

I. MINUTES OF MEETING HELD AT LOS ANGELES, JULY, 1907

Monday, July 8.—This session was called for 9:30 A. M., which proved too early an hour in N. E. A. convention week. A small number held an interesting round-table discussion at Symphony Hall, 232 South Hill St.

Several names were proposed for active membership, but owing to lack of data required by the by-law governing application and nomination for membership, the names were postponed for final action at the Washington meeting in February, 1908.

Wednesday, July 10.—At 2:30 P. M. about 100 people gathered at Symphony Hall, though a small proportion of these were members of the Society. The discussions were all on some phases of the relation of the kindergarten to primary education, and were interesting and excellent in character.

Those who took leading parts in the discussion were Ossian H. Lang, editor of the *New York School Journal;* Miss Isabel Lawrence, State Normal School, St. Cloud, Minn.; Miss Emma C. Davis, supervisor primary education, Cleveland, Ohio; and Miss Barnard, kindergartner of Oakland, Cal.

It was forcibly brought out that there is great need of the kindergartners and the primary teachers coming to a better understanding with each other regarding the work each ought to do for the child and how that work should be done so that the child may get a maximum of benefit in the primary grades from his kindergarten life and training.

II. FINANCIAL STATEMENT

This will be made at the business meeting on Wednesday, February 26.

III. THE PURPOSES, ORGANIZATION, AND WORK OF THE NATIONAL SOCIETY FOR THE SCIENTIFIC STUDY OF EDUCATION

Origin.—The National Society for the Scientific Study of Education (formerly The National Herbart Society for the Scientific Study of Education) was organized at the Denver meeting of the National Educational Association in 1895. It was one of several characteristic movements in the history of education in the United States during the last decade of the nineteenth century. It was born on the one hand of a serious and deep-felt need of advancing the status of the science and art of teaching, and on the other hand of the progressive energy and earnestness of a group of the younger American educators. These leaders are well represented by the members of the first executive committee which held office from 1895 to 1899. They were Charles DeGarmo, president; Nicholas Murray Butler, John Dewey, Wilbur S. Jackman, Elmer E. Brown, Frank M. McMurry, Levi Seeley, C. C. Van Liew; and Charles A. McMurry, secretary. In 1901 the society was organized under its present name with plans and purposes somewhat modified and extended.

Purposes.—During its first stage the National Society "was organized for the aggressive discussion and spread of educational doctrines." It desired to draw into its membership all teachers, students of education, and citizens who wish to keep abreast of the best thought and practice in education. During the second stage the original purposes have been continued, but some distinctive characteristics have been added. The present purposes may be briefly stated as follows:

1. To work toward a sound philosophic and scientific basis for educational thought and practice.

2. In connection with "1" to secure a union of the motive and spirit of both scientist and artist in all the work of the teacher.

3. To carry on study and investigation of current educational problems in a truly scientific spirit and in accordance with principles of scientific method.

4. To secure thoughtful, stimulating, and aggressive discussion of studies brought before the Society in its *Yearbook*.

5. To publish in its *Yearbook* a body of valuable literature on topics of current and permanent interest in education, and to give from time to time the status of educational opinion and practice touching some special field or problem.

6. To emphasize the idea that problems arising from one's immediate work are usually the best starting-points for a study of education.

7. To promote the spirit and secure the advantages of co-operative fellowship in the work of education.

Membership.—Any person who will actively work for the above purposes is eligible to active membership. Active members have all the privileges and share the responsibilities of conducting the work of the Society. Active membership fee is $3 a year. Application for active membership may be made through any active member or officer of the Society.

Any person in sympathy with the above purposes, and who desires to keep in touch with the Society's work may become an associate member by paying $1 a year. Associate members get the *Yearbook,* circulars of information, etc., free, and have the privilege of attending meetings of the Society. Anyone wishing the publications regularly will find it a convenience and an economy to enroll as an associate member.

It is a by-law of the Society that any member wishing to discontinue membership shall so notify the secretary.

All fees and dues are payable to the secretary at the beginning of each year.

Meetings.—Two meetings are held each year; one in February at the time of the meeting of the Department of Superintendence, the other in July in connection with the annual convention of the National Education Association.

Yearbooks.—The Society's *Yearbook* is issued in two parts, Part I being sent to members a few weeks before the February meeting, and Part II shortly before the meeting in July. The *Yearbooks* are sent out in advance of the meetings to enable members to study them in preparation for discussion; thus discussion of greater effectiveness and value is assured.

The *Yearbooks* of the Society constitute a body of educational literature of acknowledged worth. The most of this literature is of permanent value to teachers. Some of it is almost indispensable to libraries and students of education. The *Yearbooks* are now bound up in sets, each covering five years, and can be had for the cost of associate membership for period covered.

Present problems.—There are several studies now before the Society:

1. Prof. Ellwood P. Cubberley's able monograph on the certification of teachers is being followed up by the work of a strong com-

mittee to promote standards and better administration of certification of teachers in the United States.

2. The work of the committee on vocational studies for college entrance will be continued. The colleges and high schools now feel the need of establishing some standards and schedules of entrance-credit valuation for the various vocational courses in secondary schools.

3. The study of the relation of kindergarten and primary education will be supplemented. The further problem is to show rather specifically what there is or ought to be in kindergarten education that the primary teacher ought to utilize in the elementary school to the child's greatest advantage.

4. The forthcoming *Yearbook* will present a study from data of wide range and careful selection concerning the relation of superintendents and principals to the improvement of their teachers. This study will especially show conditions and how this problem is met in cities where progressive superintendents have been seriously at work to find satisfactory solution of the problem. This *Yearbook* will be discussed at the Washington meeting in February, 1908.

5. The problem of secondary industrial education in the United States will be studied and presented in an early issue of the *Yearbook*. This phase of education has come to be looked upon as a national problem, both from the international outlook regarding the commercial merits of American products, and in the light of the great importance of progressive economic efficiency in the rank and file of our population.

Prospective program.—For some time the policy of the Society has been to deal with now one, now another of the most important and pressing current educational problems. There has been a growing feeling, however, that such an organization ought to define some fundamental and comprehensive problem that would give permanence and continuity to its work for several years. Such a line of work is here briefly outlined in a series of questions and theses as a basis for discussion:

1. What ideals of life (personal and institutional) in America are or ought to be national? This will call for a profound study of American life, historical and contemporary. There are or can

be supreme, inspiring, commanding ideals of American life in whose process of realization will be embodied and sublimated the higher value and meaning of America's vast natural resources and the creative energies of her people. These must be clearly defined and continuously propagated. In the light of these ideals the meaning and value of all the details of life and education must be estimated.

2. What should be the aim and fundamental characteristics in American education in order that these ideals may be most surely realized in the highest possible degree? This will call for the discovery, defining, and systematic organization of the philosophic and scientific bases of education. From such basic principles (all of which must be derived from the nature, needs, and ideals of the people, and the relation of the individual and society) will be determined the subject-matter and all details of the entire educative process.

3. In what respects and to what extent should American education conform to national standards rather than local, and vice versa? This calls for a clear understanding of the fact that the national total is teeming with individualistic tendencies with their specialized energies, and that these factors are the mainsprings of progress and the safeguards of freedom; but it also calls for an understanding of the importance of governing factors that secure co-operative unity, coherence, and justice.

There is perennial need of getting back to fundamentals in the work of education, and the educational compass must always be corrected by reference to the life-needs of the people—their legitimate necessities, their worthiest ideals, and their more abundant life.

LIST OF ACTIVE MEMBERS OF THE NATIONAL SOCIETY FOR THE SCIENTIFIC STUDY OF EDUCATION

G. A. Axline, president State Normal School, Albion, Idaho.
Zonia Baber, School of Education, Chicago, Ill.
Frank P. Backman, Ohio University, Normal College, Athens, Ohio.
William C. Bagley, State Normal School, Oswego, N. Y.
R. H. Beggs, principal Whittier School, Denver, Colo.
Ezra W. Benedict, principal of high school, Warrensburg, N. Y.
Francis G. Blair, superintendent of public instruction, Springfield, Ill.
Frederick E. Bolton, State University of Iowa, Iowa City, Ia.
Frederick G. Bonser, State Normal School, Macomb, Ill.
Richard G. Boone, editor of *Education*, Yonkers, N. Y.
Mary D. Bradford, Stout Training Schools, Menomonie, Wis.
Thomas H. Briggs, Jr., State Normal School, Charleston, Ill.
Sarah C. Brooks, principal Teachers Training School, Baltimore, Md.
Stratton D. Brooks, superintendent of schools, Boston, Mass.
George A. Brown, editor *School and Home Education*, Bloomington, Ill.
John F. Brown, University of Wyoming, Laramie, Wyoming.
J. Stanley Brown, superintendent township high school, Joliet, Ill.
Martin G. Brumbaugh, superintendent of schools, Philadelphia, Pa.
William L. Bryan, president Indiana University, Bloomington, Ind.
W. J. S. Bryan, principal Central High School, St. Louis, Mo.
Edward F. Buchner, University of Alabama, University, Ala.
W. H. Burnham, Clark University, Worcester, Mass.
Elizabeth H. Bunnell, Training School for Teachers, Prospect Place, near Nostrand Ave., Brooklyn, N. Y.
B. C. Caldwell, president Louisiana State Normal School, Natchitoches, La.
Arthur D. Call, district superintendent, Hartford, Conn.
I. I. Cammack, principal Central High School, Kansas City, Mo.
John W. Carr, superintendent of schools, Dayton, O.
Clarence F. Carroll, superintendent of schools, Rochester, N. Y.
C. P. Cary, state superintendent, Madison, Wis.
Charles E. Chadsey, superintendent of schools, Denver, Colo.
P. P. Claxton, University of Tennessee, Knoxville, Tenn.
John W. Cook, president State Normal School, De Kalb, Ill.
Flora J. Cooke, principal Francis W. Parker School, Chicago, Ill.
Frank W. Cooley, superintendent of schools, Evansville, Ind.
Ellwood P. Cubberley, Leland Stanford Jr. University, Stanford University, Cal.
Emma C. Davis, supervisor primary education, Cleveland, O.
W. S. Dearmont, president State Normal School, Cape Girardeau, Mo.
Charles DeGarmo, Cornell University, Ithaca, N. Y.
John Dewey, Columbia University, New York, N. Y.
Edwin G. Dexter, commissioner of education, San Juan, Porto Rico.
Richard E. Dodge, Columbia University, New York, N. Y.
Mary E. Doyle, State Normal School, Superior, Wis.
Charles B. Dyke, University of Colorado, Boulder, Colo.

Lida B. Earhart, 1230 Amsterdam Ave., New York, N. Y.
Gertrude Edmund, principal Lowell Training School, Lowell, Mass.
Edward C. Elliott, University of Wisconsin, Madison, Wis.
A. Caswell Ellis, University of Texas, Austin, Tex.
William H. Elson, superintendent of schools, Cleveland, O.
Frederick E. Farrington, University of California, Berkeley, Cal.
David Felmley, president Illinois State Normal University, Normal, Ill.
Frank A. Fitzpatrick, manager American Book Co., Boston, Mass.
A. C. Fleshman, Kentucky State College, Lexington, Ky.
George M. Forbes, Rochester University, Rochester, N. Y.
J. M. H. Frederick, superintendent of schools, Lakewood, O.
J. M. Frost, superintendent of schools, Muskegon, Mich.
J. Montgomery Gambrill, assistant superintendent of education, Baltimore, Md.
Wilbur F. Gordy, superintendent of schools, Springfield, Mass.
Maximilian P. E. Groszmann, director Groszmann School, Plainfield, N. J.
W. H. Hailman, Chicago Normal School, Chicago, Ill.
Reuben Post Halleck, principal Boys' High School, Louisville, Ky.
Cora M. Hamilton, State Normal School, Macomb, Ill.
Paul H. Hanus, Harvard University, Cambridge, Mass.
Ada VanStone Harris, supervisor kindergartens and primary education, Rochester, N. Y.
L. D. Harvey, superintendent Stout Training Schools, Menomonie, Wis.
W. H. Hatch, superintendent of schools, Oak Park, Ill.
Josephine W. Heerman, principal Whittier School, Kansas City, Mo.
Hermon C. Henderson, State Normal School, Milwaukee, Wis.
J. W. Henninger, 6433 Monroe Ave., Chicago, Ill.
Cheesman A. Herrick, Central High School, Philadelphia, Pa.
Warren E. Hicks, assistant superintendent of schools, Cleveland, O.
Patty Smith Hill, instructor kindergarten supervision, Teachers College, New York, N. Y.
Horace H. Hollister, high-school visitor, University of Illinois, Urbana, Ill.
Manfred J. Holmes, Illinois State Normal University, Normal, Ill.
Walter Ballou Jacobs, Brown University, Providence, R. I.
Benjamin B. James, Millikin University, Decatur, Ill.
Jeremiah W. Jenks, Cornell University, Ithaca, N. Y.
Lewis H. Jones, president State Normal College, Ypsilanti, Mich.
John A. H. Keith, president State Normal School, Oshkosh, Wis.
Calvin N. Kendall, superintendent of schools, Indianapolis, Ind.
Charles H. Keyes, supervisor of schools, Hartford, Conn.
John R. Kirk, president State Normal School, Kirksville, Mo.
W. H. Kirk, superintendent of schools, East Cleveland, O.
Henry E. Kratz, superintendent of schools, Calumet, Mich.
Maria Kraus-Boelte, principal Kraus' Seminary for Kindergartners, New York City.
Ossian H. Lang, editor *School Journal,* New York, N. Y.
Isabel Lawrence, State Normal School, St. Cloud, Minn.
Homer P. Lewis, superintendent of schools, Worcester, Mass.
Anna E. Logan, Miami University, Oxford, O.
L. C. Lord, president State Normal School, Charleston, Ill.
Charles D. Lowry, district superintendent of schools, Chicago, Ill.

G. W. A. Luckey, University of Nebraska, Lincoln, Neb.
Herman T. Lukens, Francis W. Parker School, Chicago, Ill.
E. O. Lyte, president State Normal School, Millersville, Pa.
John A. MacVannel, Columbia University, New York, N. Y.
Frank A. Manny, Ethical Culture School, Central Park West and 63rd St., New York, N. Y.
William H. Maxwell, superintendent of schools, New York, N. Y.
Arthur Newell McCallum, superintendent of schools, Austin, Tex.
W. J. McConathy, principal Normal School, Louisville, Ky.
C. M. McDaniel, superintendent of schools, Hammond, Ind.
Charles McKenny, president State Normal School, Milwaukee, Wis.
Charles A. McMurry, State Normal School, De Kalb, Ill.
Frank M. McMurry, Teachers College, Columbia University, New York, N. Y.
I. C. McNeill, superintendent of schools, Memphis, Tenn.
Irving E. Miller, State Normal School, Milwaukee, Wis.
G. R. Miller, State Normal College, Greeley, Colo.
William A. Millis, superintendent of schools, Crawfordsville, Ind.
J. F. Millspaugh, president State Normal School, Los Angeles, Cal.
Will S. Monroe, State Normal School, Westfield, Mass.
George A. Newton, superintendent of schools, Greenville, Tex.
Theodore B. Noss, president State Normal School, California, Pa.
A. S. Olin, University of Kansas, Lawrence, Kan.
M. V. O'Shea, University of Wisconsin, Madison, Wis.
Frank H. Palmer, editor of *Education,* Boston, Mass.
Bertha Payne, head kindergartner, School of Education, Chicago, Ill.
George D. Pickels, Louisiana State Normal School, Natchitoches, La.
Rosalie Pollock, supervisor primary education, Salt Lake City, Utah.
R. R. Reeder, superintendent New York Orphan Asylum, Hastings-on-Hudson, N. Y.
J. F. Reigart, principal Public School No. 89, New York City, Yonkers, N. Y.
Emily J. Rice, School of Education, University of Chicago, Chicago, Ill.
C. R. Richards, director manual training, Columbia University, New York, N. Y.
R. N. Roark, president State Normal College, Richmond, Ky.
Stuart H. Rowe, Brooklyn Training School for Teachers, Brooklyn, N. Y.
James E. Russell, dean of Teachers College, New York, N. Y.
Myron T. Scudder, principal State Normal School, New Paltz, N. Y.
Homer H. Seerley, president State Normal School, Cedar Falls, Ia.
Burgess Shank, State Normal School, Valley City, S. D.
James J. Sheppard, principal High School of Commerce, New York, N. Y.
Waite A. Shoemaker, president, State Normal School, St. Cloud, Minn.
Herbert M. Slauson, superintendent of schools, Ann Arbor, Mich.
David E. Smith, Teachers College, Columbia University, New York, N. Y.
David S. Snedden, Teachers College, Columbia University, New York, N. Y.
Z. X. Snyder, president State Normal School, Greeley, Colo.
F. Louis Soldan, superintendent of instruction, St. Louis, Mo.
John K. Stableton, superintendent of schools, Bloomington, Ill.
Edwin D. Starbuck, Earlham College, Richmond, Ind.
William E. Stark, principal Ethical Culture High School, New York, N. Y.
George D. Strayer, Teachers College, Columbia University, New York, N. Y.

W. S. Sutton, University of Texas, Austin, Tex.
Henry Suzzallo, Teachers College, Columbia University, New York, N. Y.
Joseph S. Taylor, district superintendent of schools, New York, N. Y.
Edward L. Thorndike, Columbia University, New York, N. Y.
Charles H. Thurber, editor, Ginn & Company, Boston, Mass.
A. W. Tressler, inspector of schools, University of Wisconsin, Madison, Wis.
C. C. Van Liew, president State Normal School, Chico, Cal.
James H. Van Sickle, superintendent of schools, Baltimore, Md.
Elmer W. Walker, superintendent State School for the Deaf, Delavan, Wis.
A. S. Whitney, University of Michigan, Ann Arbor, Mich.
John J. Wilkinson, Elmhurst, Ill.
J. N. Wilkinson, Emporia, Kan.

CPSIA information can be obtained
at www.ICGtesting.com
Printed in the USA
BVHW04*1047170918
527708BV00015B/1932/P